AL FRESCO
EATS

AL FRESCO EATS

COLLINS & BROWN

The Good Housekeeping website is
www.goodhousekeeping.co.uk

ISBN 978-1-908449-94-8

A catalogue record for this book is available from
the British Library.

Reproduction by Dot Gradations Ltd, UK
Printed and bound by
1010 Printing International Ltd, China

This book can be ordered direct from the publisher.
Contact the marketing department, but try your
bookshop first.

www.anovabooks.com

NOTES
Both metric and imperial measures are given for
the recipes. Follow either set of measures, not a
mixture of both, as they are not interchangeable.

All spoon measures are level.
1 tsp = 5ml spoon; 1 tbsp = 15ml spoon.

Ovens and grills must be preheated to the specified
temperature.

Medium eggs should be used except where
otherwise specified. Free-range eggs are
recommended.

Note that some recipes contain raw or lightly
cooked eggs. The young, elderly, pregnant women
and anyone with an immune-deficiency disease
should avoid these because of the slight risk
of salmonella.

Contents

Super Salads

Herb Vinegar

To make 600ml (1 pint), you will need:
25g (1oz) fresh herbs, plus extra sprigs
for bottling, 600ml (1 pint) red or
white wine vinegar.

1 Put the herbs and vinegar into a
   pan and bring to the boil. Pour into
   a heatproof bowl, cover and leave
   overnight.
2 Strain through a muslin-lined
   sieve and bottle with herb sprigs.
   Store for one week before using.

Garlic, Soy and Honey

To make about 100ml (3½fl oz), you
will need:
1 garlic clove, crushed, 2 tsp each soy
sauce and honey, 1 tbsp cider vinegar,
4 tbsp olive oil, freshly ground black
pepper.

1 Put the garlic in a small bowl. Add
   the soy sauce, honey, vinegar and
   olive oil, season to taste with
   pepper and whisk together
   thoroughly.
2 If not using, store in a cool place
   and whisk briefly before using.

Classic Coleslaw

To make about 175ml (6fl oz), you will
need:
2½ tbsp red wine vinegar, 125ml (4fl
oz) olive oil, 1 tbsp Dijon mustard, salt
and freshly ground black pepper.

1 Pour the vinegar into a large
   screw-topped jar. Add the olive oil
   and mustard and season with salt
   and ground black pepper. Screw
   on the lid and shake well.
2 Combine with the coleslaw
   ingredients and chill in the fridge
   until needed.

Sun-dried Tomato

To make about 100ml (3½fl oz), you will need:
2 sun-dried tomatoes in oil, drained, 2 tbsp oil from sun-dried tomato jar, 2 tbsp red wine vinegar, 1 garlic clove, 1 tbsp sun-dried tomato paste, a pinch of sugar (optional), 2 tbsp extra virgin olive oil, salt and freshly ground black pepper.

1 Put the sun-dried tomatoes and oil, the vinegar, garlic and tomato paste into a blender or food processor. Add the sugar, if you like.
2 With the motor running, pour the oil through the feeder tube and whiz briefly to make a fairly thick dressing. Season to taste with salt and ground black pepper. If not using store in a cool place and whisk briefly before using.

Fruit Vinegar

To make 600ml (1 pint), you will need:
450g (1lb) raspberries and blackberries, plus extra for bottling, 600ml (1 pint) red wine vinegar.

1 Put the fruit into a bowl and, using the back of a spoon, break it up, then add the vinegar. Cover and leave to stand for three days, stirring now and then.
2 Strain through a muslin-lined sieve and bottle with extra fruits. Store for two weeks before using.

2

Grated Beetroot Salad

Hands-on time: 15 minutes

3 large carrots
500g (1lb 2oz) raw beetroot
finely grated zest and juice
  of 1 large orange
1½ tbsp runny honey
1 eating apple
50g (2oz) walnuts, roughly chopped
a few caperberries
a small handful of fresh flat-leafed
  parsley, roughly chopped
salt and freshly ground black pepper

1 Peel and coarsely grate the carrots and put into one half of a serving bowl. Wearing kitchen gloves to stop your hands getting stained, peel and coarsely grate the beetroot, then put into the other half of the bowl.

2 Mix the orange zest and juice, honey and some seasoning together in a small bowl.

3 Finely dice the apple (keeping the skin on) and scatter over the grated vegetables, together with the walnuts, caperberries and parsley. Drizzle the dressing over and serve.

SAVE TIME

Prepare the salad to the end of step 1 up to 1 hour before you plan to eat. Cover and chill the vegetables. Cover the dressing and keep at room temperature, then complete the recipe to serve.

Serves 6

Classic Coleslaw

Hands-on time: 15 minutes

¼ each medium red and white
   cabbage, shredded

1 carrot, grated

20g (¾oz) fresh flat-leafed parsley,
   finely chopped

For the dressing

1½ tbsp red wine vinegar

4 tbsp olive oil

½ tsp Dijon mustard

salt and freshly ground black pepper

1 To make the dressing, put the vinegar into a small bowl, add the oil and mustard, season well with salt and ground black pepper and mix well.

2 Put the cabbage and carrot into a large bowl and toss to mix well. Add the parsley.

3 Mix the dressing again, pour over the cabbage mixture and toss well to coat.

Serves 6

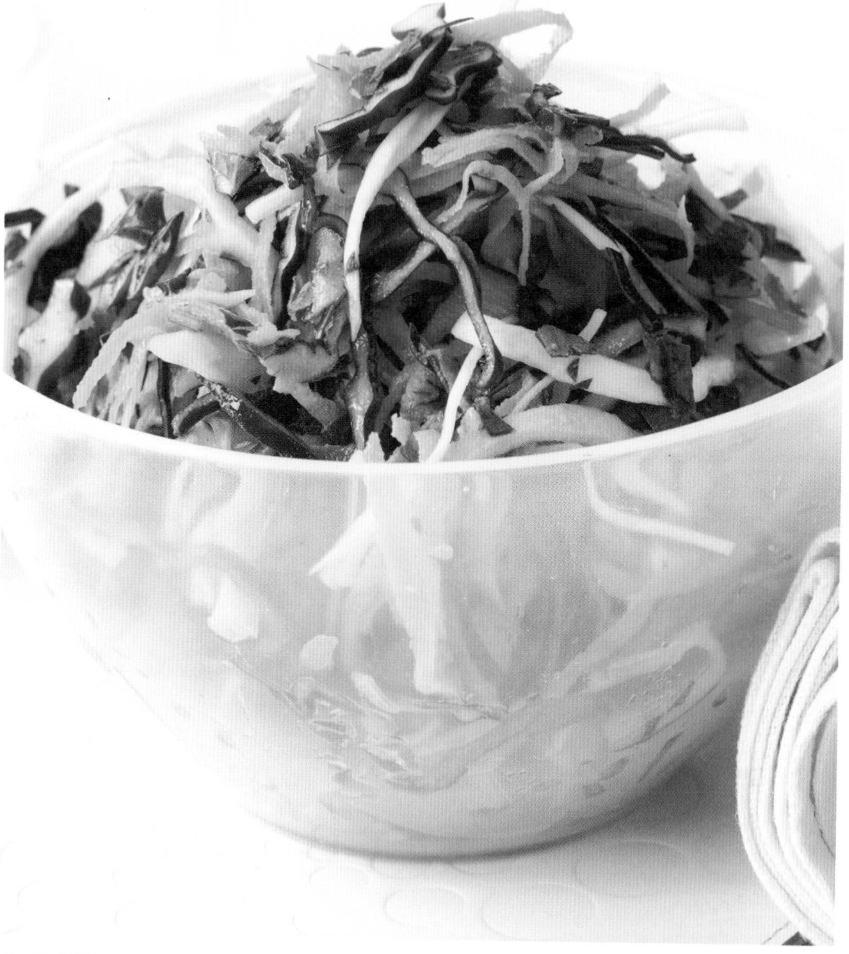

Mediterranean Salad

Hands-on time: 15 minutes

2 × 410g cans chickpeas, drained
  and rinsed

4 tomatoes, roughly chopped

1 red onion, thinly sliced

2 small courgettes, cut into ribbons
  with a peeler

160g pack hot-smoked salmon,
  skinned and flaked

50g (2oz) raisins

1 tbsp wholegrain mustard

1 tsp runny honey

1 tsp white wine vinegar

2 tbsp extra virgin olive oil

a large handful of fresh basil

2 tbsp pumpkin seeds

salt and freshly ground black pepper

1 Combine the chickpeas, tomatoes, onion, courgettes, salmon and raisins in a large bowl.

2 Whisk together the mustard, honey, vinegar, oil and some seasoning in a small jug. Pour the dressing over the salad and toss to coat. Sprinkle with the basil and pumpkin seeds and serve immediately.

Serves 4

Pasta and Avocado Salad

TAKE
5

Hands-on time: 10 minutes

2 tbsp mayonnaise

2 tbsp pesto

2 ripe avocados, halved, stoned, peeled
and cut into cubes

225g (8oz) cooked pasta shapes,
cooled

a few fresh basil leaves to garnish

1 Mix the mayonnaise with the pesto
and avocados, then stir into the
pasta. If the dressing is too thick,
dilute with a little water (use the
pasta cooking water if you have it).

2 Scatter a few basil leaves over the
salad and serve as a starter.

SAVE TIME

Cook the pasta up to a day ahead
and leave to cool, then chill.
Complete the recipe when ready
to serve – cut avocado flesh will
discolour if left for any length
of time.

Serves 4

White Bean Salad

½ tbsp red wine vinegar

2 tbsp extra virgin olive oil

½ red cabbage

2 courgettes

410g can cannellini beans, drained and rinsed

410g can butter beans, drained and rinsed

½ red onion, finely chopped

100g (3½oz) stale unsliced bread, torn into small chunks

125g ball low-fat mozzarella, torn into small pieces

a handful of fresh basil leaves, chopped

salt and freshly ground black pepper

1 Whisk together the vinegar, oil, plenty of seasoning and a splash of water in a small bowl to make a dressing.

2 Cut out and discard the tough core from the cabbage, then finely shred the leaves and put into a large serving bowl. Using a y-shaped peeler, peel the courgettes into ribbons and add to the cabbage bowl. Add the remaining ingredients and dressing and toss well to combine. Serve.

Serves 4

Greek Pasta Salad

Hands-on time: 10 minutes
Cooking time: 20 minutes

3 tbsp olive oil
2 tbsp lemon juice
150g (5oz) cooked pasta shapes,
   cooled
75g (3oz) feta, crumbled
3 tomatoes, roughly chopped
2 tbsp small pitted black olives
½ cucumber, roughly chopped
1 small red onion, finely sliced
salt and freshly ground black pepper
freshly chopped parsley and lemon
   zest to garnish
crusty bread to serve

SAVE TIME

Cook the pasta up to a day ahead.
Cool, then chill. Complete the
recipe to serve.

1 Mix the oil and lemon juice together
   in a salad bowl, then add the pasta,
   feta, tomatoes, olives, cucumber and
   onion. Season and stir to mix.
2 Garnish with chopped parsley
   and lemon zest and serve with
   crusty bread.

Serves 2

Take 5 Quick Salad Dressings

Mustard

To make about 100ml (3½fl oz), you will need:
1 tbsp wholegrain mustard, juice of
½ lemon, 6 tbsp extra virgin olive oil,
salt and freshly ground black pepper.

1 Put the mustard, lemon juice and
   oil into a small bowl and whisk
   together. Season to taste with salt
   and ground black pepper.
2 If not using immediately, store in a
   cool place and whisk briefly before
   using.

Mint Yogurt

To make about 175ml (6fl oz), you will
need:
150g (5oz) Greek yogurt, 3–4 tbsp
freshly chopped mint leaves,
2 tbsp extra virgin olive oil, salt
and freshly ground black pepper.

1 Put the yogurt in a bowl and add
   the mint and olive oil. Season to
   taste.
2 If not using immediately, store in a
   cool place and use within one day.

Blue Cheese

To make 100ml (3½fl oz), you will
need:
50g (2oz) Roquefort cheese, 2 tbsp
low-fat yogurt, 1 tbsp white wine
vinegar, 5 tbsp extra virgin olive oil,
salt and freshly ground black pepper.

1 Crumble the cheese into a food
   processor and add the yogurt,
   vinegar and oil. Whiz for 1 minute
   until thoroughly combined.
   Season to taste with salt and
   ground black pepper.
2 Store in a cool place and use
   within one day.

Lemon and Parsley

To make about 100ml (3½fl oz), you will need:

juice of ½ lemon, 6 tbsp extra virgin olive oil, 4 tbsp freshly chopped flat-leafed parsley, salt and freshly ground black pepper.

1. Put the lemon juice, oil and parsley into a medium bowl and whisk together. Season to taste with salt and ground black pepper.
2. If not using immediately, store in a cool place and whisk briefly before using.

Chilli Lime

To make 125ml (4fl oz), you will need:

¼ red chilli, seeded and finely chopped (see Safety Tip, page 52), 1 garlic clove, crushed, 1cm (½in) piece fresh root ginger, peeled and finely grated, juice of 1½ large limes, 50ml (2fl oz) olive oil, 1½ tbsp light muscovado sugar, 2 tbsp fresh coriander leaves, 2 tbsp fresh mint leaves.

1. Put the chilli, garlic, ginger, lime juice, oil and sugar into a food processor or blender and whiz for 10 seconds to combine. Add the coriander and mint leaves and whiz together for 5 seconds to chop roughly.
2. Store in a cool place and use within two days.

Provençale Tuna and Pepper Salad

Hands-on time: 15 minutes
Cooking time: about 10 minutes

400g (14oz) new potatoes, halved
  if large

200g (7oz) green beans

4 medium eggs

1 tbsp extra virgin olive oil

grated zest and juice of 1 lemon

50g (2oz) black olives, pitted

300g (11oz) ready-roasted red peppers,
  cut into thick strips

185g can tuna chunks, drained

25g pack fresh basil leaves, torn

salt and freshly ground black pepper

1 Bring a medium pan of water to the boil. Add the potatoes, reduce the heat and simmer for 10 minutes until tender, adding the beans for the final 4 minutes of cooking. Drain and leave to steam-dry until needed.

2 Meanwhile, bring a small pan of water to the boil, add the eggs and simmer for 8 minutes. Drain and run them under cold water. Shell and quarter the eggs, then put them to one side. In a small bowl, mix together the oil, lemon zest and juice with some seasoning.

3 Put the potatoes, green beans, olives, pepper strips, tuna and basil leaves into a large serving dish. Add the dressing and gently toss through (using your hands is best). Garnish with the egg quarters and serve immediately.

Classic Salad Dressings

Basic Vinaigrette

To make about 300ml (½ pint), you will need:
100ml (3½fl oz) extra virgin olive oil, 100ml (3½fl oz) grapeseed oil, 50ml (2fl oz) white wine vinegar, a pinch each of sugar and English mustard powder, 1 garlic clove, crushed (optional), salt and freshly ground black pepper.

1 Put both oils, the vinegar, sugar, mustard powder and garlic, if you like, into a large screw-topped jar. Tighten the lid and shake well. Season to taste with salt and ground black pepper.
2 If not using immediately, store in a cool place and shake briefly before using.

Balsamic Dressing

To make about 100ml (3½fl oz), you will need:
2 tbsp balsamic vinegar, 4 tbsp extra virgin olive oil, salt and freshly ground black pepper.

1 Whisk the vinegar and oil in a small bowl. Season to taste with salt and ground black pepper.
2 If not using immediately, store in a cool place and whisk briefly before using.

SAVE EFFORT

To help it emulsify easily, add 1 tsp cold water to the dressing.
To get a really good emulsion, shake the dressing vigorously in a screw-topped jar.

French Dressing

To make 100ml (3½fl oz), you will need:
1 tsp Dijon mustard, a pinch of sugar, 1 tbsp red or white wine vinegar, 6 tbsp extra virgin olive oil, salt and freshly ground black pepper.

1 Put the mustard, sugar and vinegar into a small bowl and season with salt and ground black pepper. Whisk thoroughly until well combined, then gradually whisk in the oil until thoroughly combined.
2 If not using immediately, store in a cool place and whisk briefly before using.

French Dressing variations

Herb Dressing Use half the mustard, replace the vinegar with lemon juice, and add 2 tbsp freshly chopped herbs, such as parsley, chervil and chives.
Garlic Dressing Add 1 crushed garlic clove to the dressing at step 2.

Caesar

To make about 150ml (¼ pint), you will need:
1 medium egg, 1 garlic clove, juice of ½ lemon, 2 tsp Dijon mustard, 1 tsp balsamic vinegar, 150ml (¼ pint) sunflower oil, salt and freshly ground black pepper.

1 Put the egg, garlic, lemon juice, mustard and vinegar into a food processor and whiz until smooth then, with the motor running, gradually add the oil and whiz until smooth. Season with salt and ground black pepper.
2 Cover and chill in the fridge for up to three days.

Couscous and Haddock Salad

Hands-on time: 15 minutes
Cooking time: 15 minutes

175g (6oz) couscous
125g (4oz) cooked smoked haddock, flaked
50g (2oz) cooked peas
a pinch of curry powder
2 spring onions, sliced
1 tbsp freshly chopped flat-leafed parsley
1 small hard-boiled egg, chopped
2 tbsp olive oil
2 tsp lemon juice
salt and freshly ground black pepper

1 Cook the couscous according to the pack instructions. Drain if necessary.
2 Mix the couscous with the smoked haddock, peas, curry powder, spring onions, parsley and egg.
3 Toss with the oil, lemon juice and plenty of salt and ground black pepper to taste, then serve.

Serves 4

Melon and Chorizo Salad

Hands-on time: 10 minutes
Cooking time: about 8 minutes

1 cantaloupe melon
75ml (3fl oz) balsamic vinegar
1 tbsp runny honey
75g (3oz) chorizo, in one piece, skinned
1 tbsp oil
1 punnet of cress, trimmed
crusty bread to serve (optional)

1 Halve the melon, then spoon out and discard the seeds. Cut each half into three wedges, then cut the skin off each wedge and chill the wedges until needed.

2 Put the vinegar and honey into a small pan and simmer gently for 5 minutes until syrupy. Leave to cool.

3 Cut the chorizo into small cubes. Heat the oil in a small frying pan and add the sausage cubes and fry for 3 minutes until the chorizo is golden. Strain into a small bowl and put the oil and chorizo to one side.

4 Put a melon wedge on each of six small plates, then sprinkle with some of the fried chorizo and the cress. Finally, drizzle the chorizo oil and balsamic glaze over each plate. Serve immediately, with crusty bread, if you like.

SAVE TIME

Prepare the salad to the end of step 3 up to 2 hours before you plan to eat. Cover the balsamic glaze and chorizo oil and keep at room temperature. Cover the melon and chorizo and chill in the fridge. Allow the chorizo to come up to room temperature before completing the recipe to serve.

Serves 6

Broad Bean and Feta Salad

Hands-on time: 10 minutes
Cooking time: 5 minutes

225g (8oz) podded broad beans (see Save Time)
100g (3½oz) feta, chopped
2 tbsp freshly chopped mint
2 tbsp extra virgin olive oil
a squeeze of lemon juice
salt and freshly ground black pepper
lemon wedges to serve (optional)

1 Cook the beans in salted boiling water for 3–5 minutes until tender. Drain, then plunge them into cold water and drain again. Remove their skins, if you like (see Save Time).
2 Tip the beans into a bowl, add the feta, mint, oil and a squeeze of lemon juice. Season well with salt and ground black pepper and toss together. Serve with lemon wedges, if you like.

SAVE TIME

For this quantity of broad beans, you will need to buy about 750g (1½lb) beans in pods. Choose small pods, as the beans will be young and will have a better flavour than bigger, older beans.
Very young broad beans, less than 7.5cm (3in) long, can be cooked in their pods and eaten whole. Pod older beans and skin them to remove the outer coat, which toughens with age. To do this, slip the beans out of their skins after blanching. Allow about 250g (9oz) weight of whole beans in pods per person.

Serves 2

Pasta, Salami and Tapenade Salad

TAKE 5

Hands-on time: 5 minutes

3 × 225g tubs pasta salad in tomato sauce
75g (3oz) pepper salami, shredded
3 tbsp black olive tapenade paste
3 tbsp freshly chopped chives
salt and freshly ground black pepper

SAVE EFFORT

For a simple tomato and basil salad, omit the spring onions and pinenuts, and reduce the quantity of dressing by one-third.

1 Turn the pasta salad into a large bowl, add the salami, tapenade and chives. Toss everything together and season with ground black pepper. Check for seasoning before adding salt – the tapenade may have made the salad salty enough. Pile the salad into a large serving bowl.
2 If not being served straight away, store in a cool place, but not chilled, until needed.

Serves 4

Waldorf Salad

450g (1lb) eating apples
juice of ½ lemon
1 tsp sugar
150ml (¼ pint) mayonnaise
1 lettuce
½ head of celery, sliced
50g (2oz) walnut pieces, chopped
a few walnut halves to garnish
  (optional)

1 Peel and core the apples, slice one and dice the rest. Dip the slices into lemon juice to prevent discoloration. Combine the lemon juice, sugar and 1 tbsp mayonnaise and toss the diced apples in the mixture. Leave to stand for about 30 minutes.

2 Just before serving, line a salad bowl with lettuce leaves. Add the celery, walnuts and remaining mayonnaise to the diced apples and toss together. Spoon into the salad bowl and garnish with the apple slices and a few whole walnuts, if you like.

Serves 4

Salad Caprese

3 × 150g balls mozzarella, drained
1kg (2¼lb) very ripe tomatoes, sliced
  into rounds
extra virgin olive oil to drizzle
a small handful of fresh basil leaves,
  roughly shredded
sea salt and freshly ground
  black pepper

1 Slice the mozzarella into rounds and
  layer with the tomato slices on a
  serving plate.
2 Drizzle with the oil, season with
  salt and ground black pepper and
  scatter the basil over.

Serves 4

Tomato and Onion Salad

Hands-on time: 15 minutes, plus standing

500g (1lb 2oz) baby plum tomatoes, halved

1 bunch of spring onions, sliced

500g (1lb 2oz) plum tomatoes, sliced lengthways

a handful of fresh basil leaves, roughly torn, plus sprigs to garnish

2 beef tomatoes, about 450g (1lb) in total, sliced

100g (3½oz) pinenuts, toasted

250g (9oz) medium tomatoes, cut into wedges

salt and freshly ground black pepper

For the dressing

100ml (3½fl oz) extra virgin olive oil

50ml (2fl oz) balsamic vinegar

a pinch of golden caster sugar

1 First make the dressing. Put the oil, vinegar and sugar into a screw-topped jar, then season generously with salt and ground black pepper. Shake well to combine.

2 Layer the baby plum tomatoes, spring onions, plum tomatoes, basil, beef tomatoes, pinenuts and, finally, the medium tomatoes in a shallow serving bowl, seasoning each layer with salt and ground black pepper.

3 Drizzle the dressing over the salad and leave to stand for 1 hour to allow the flavours to mingle. Garnish with basil sprigs to serve.

SAVE EFFORT

For a simple tomato and basil salad, omit the spring onions and pinenuts, and reduce the quantity of dressing by one-third.

Serves 4

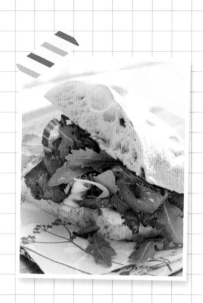

Grills and Barbecues

Planning Your Barbecue

What could be better on a hot summer's day than a barbecue? Food always smells particularly appetising when it's cooking in the open air. But before you invite your friends round, take a little time to make a plan, so you can enjoy yourself while you cook.

Choose your fuel

- Lumpwood charcoal or good-quality charcoal briquettes give out a good heat and cook evenly.
- One of the easiest and least messy barbecue fuels are 'ready in the bag' charcoal briquettes, available from petrol stations and supermarkets. They are very simple to use – just place the bag on the barbecue and light with a match.
- Make sure you choose charcoal from sustainable sources, such as brands accredited by the Forest Stewardship Council (FSC).
- Aromatic wood chips and flavourings are best used with a hooded barbecue so that the smoke permeates the food during cooking; in an open barbecue the flavour just burns away.
- A gas barbecue can be expensive to buy, but is easy to control.

SAVE TIME

If the weather lets you down, most of the recipes in this chapter can be cooked under the grill or in a ridged griddle pan. Preheat the grill for about 10 minutes, the griddle pan for 5–10 minutes – and remember that cooking times may be a bit longer than on a barbecue.

Get set

Before you start, make sure the barbecue is clean; a wire brush and warm soapy water should do the trick. If the grill looks particularly grimy, soak it in a solution of soda crystals, scrub with a metal scourer, then rinse and dry well. Make sure you have enough fuel. A layer of sand in the drip tray of a gas barbecue will make cleaning up much easier.

Next, gather together chopping boards, serving dishes and glasses, cook's knives, basting brushes, tongs, a fork, spatula and a turner, oven gloves, kitchen foil, kitchen paper, paper napkins, water spray, a bucket of water or a fire blanket (to douse any flames), corkscrew and bottle opener.

SAVE EFFORT

A good set of tools will help your barbecue run smoothly, making it easy to grip and turn food on the grill. Look for dishwasher-safe stainless steel utensils: tongs, a fork and a turner.

A hinged, double-sided grill rack will help turn delicate food such as fish, which can easily fall apart. Larger grill racks are perfect for turning lots of food over at once.

These are available from kitchen departments, garden centres and large supermarkets.

Health and safety hints

· Position your barbecue on solid level ground, away from buildings or fences. Avoid windy areas. Don't leave food on the barbecue unattended.

· Keep children and pets away from the barbecue.

· Tie back long hair and don't wear trailing sleeves or scarves; wear an apron to protect your clothes.

· Use extra-long matches when lighting the fire, so that your fingers don't get burned.

· Use oven gloves and long-handled barbecue tools for turning food.

· Have a bucket of water or a fire blanket to hand to douse the flames if they get out of control, and a spray water bottle to help stop grease flare-ups.

· Leave the embers until completely cold before throwing them away; embers that look grey may still be hot. Cover with a lid, if available, and leave overnight.

The Perfect Barbecue

Have some nibbles ready so that your guests don't get too hungry while waiting for food to be cooked. Raw vegetables such as carrots, celery and cucumber, cut into strips, with one or two simple dips or salsas, are ideal. and easy to prepare.

Ready to cook

- Long metal skewers are useful; wooden or bamboo skewers are an attractive alternative, but remember to soak them in a bowl of cold water for 20-30 minutes before you use them, to prevent them from burning.
- Take ingredients out of the fridge about 30 minutes before cooking to ensure the food cooks quickly and evenly. This is especially important for chicken and pork, which should always be cooked through.
- To prevent food from sticking on the barbecue, grease the grill rack with a little sunflower oil after heating for 10 minutes.
- Brush food with oil or baste with any remaining marinade to keep it moist while cooking.
- Cook fish and meat separately – allow the barbecue to burn freely for a few minutes between fish and meat to remove any food traces.
- Ensure food is cooked thoroughly, especially pork and poultry. It might look cooked on the outside, but may still be raw inside. Test by piercing with a thin skewer: if the juices run clear the meat is cooked through; if not, put back on the barbecue or grill for a few minutes. Or use a meat thermometer.
- Resist the urge to poke or prod food too much – this will help preserve its flavour and juices.
- Turn only once during cooking.

Light your fire

- Light a charcoal barbecue 30-40 minutes before you want to use it so that there are no flames.
- Arrange firelighters in the bottom of the barbecue. Pile the charcoal in a pyramid 5-7.5cm (2-3in) high over the top. Light the firelighters with a taper or long match and leave them

to get the fire started.

- When the coals are burning strongly, spread them out in an even layer and leave until they are glowing red at night or lightly covered in whitish ash in daylight.
- You must use enough fuel to cook all your food and that the temperature is right. Always get the coals to white heat – glowing and covered with white ash, with no black showing and no flames, as these will burn rather than cook the meat.
- To test how hot the barbecue is, hold your hand about 10cm (4in) above the grill rack. If you can keep your hand there for only 1–2 seconds, the coals are very hot; if you can manage 3–4 seconds the coals are medium–hot.
- When you are ready to cook, put the barbecue grid in position to heat up. To keep the charcoal at the right temperature, add fresh charcoal gradually around the edge. Do not add charcoal on top of the fire: it may create flames or excessive smoke.

Food hygiene

- Always cover raw poultry and meat and store in the bottom of the fridge, where it can't touch or drip on to other foods.
- Never barbecue frozen food; thaw it first.
- Raw poultry and meat contain harmful bacteria that can spread easily to anything they touch.
- Always wash your hands, kitchen surfaces, chopping boards, knives and equipment before and after handling poultry or meat.
- Use separate chopping boards for raw and cooked foods to prevent cross-contamination.
- Don't let raw poultry or meat touch other foods.
- Store raw foods in covered containers out of direct sunshine – coolboxes are perfect.
- Keep different raw foods separate and never mix together in the same marinade.
- Cook vegetarian food on a separate barbecue.

Lime and Chilli Swordfish

Hands-on time: 10 minutes, plus marinating
Cooking time: 10 minutes

1 tsp dried chilli flakes
4 tbsp olive oil
grated zest and juice of 1 lime,
    plus 1 whole lime, sliced, to serve
1 garlic clove
4 × 175g (6oz) swordfish steaks
salt and freshly ground black pepper
mixed salad to serve

1 Put the chilli flakes into a large shallow bowl. Add the olive oil, lime zest, juice and garlic and mix everything together. Add the swordfish steaks to the marinade and toss several times to coat completely. Leave to marinate for 30 minutes.

2 Preheat the barbecue or a griddle pan until hot.

3 Lift the swordfish out of the marinade, season well with salt and ground black pepper, then cook the steaks for 2 minutes on each side. Top with slices of lime and continue to cook for 1 minute or until the fish is opaque right through. Serve immediately with a mixed salad.

Serves 4

Preparing Fish and Shellfish

Fish and shellfish are perfect grilled or cooked on the barbecue, as the high heat quickly seals the succulent flesh inside a tasty outer layer.

Choosing fish

Whole fish such as sardines, red mullet, mackerel and sea bass are particularly good barbecued.

Steaks of salmon, tuna, swordfish or halibut are perfect for barbecuing – marinate them first for best results.

Thick fillets and steaks of firm white fish such as cod and halibut are suitable for grilling.

Flat fish such as sole and plaice are excellent cooked under the grill, but are too delicate to be cooked directly on the barbecue.

Prawns are ideal either grilled or barbecued. Peeled prawns should be marinated and threaded on to skewers; large prawns can be cooked in their shells – messy to eat but very tasty.

Cleaning round fish

Most fishmongers will clean fish for you, but it is very simple to clean them yourself.

1   Cut off the fins with scissors. Using the blunt edge of a knife, scrape the fish from tail to head and rinse off the loose scales. (The scaled fish should feel smooth.)
2   Insert a sharp knife at the hole towards the rear of the stomach and slit the skin up to the gills. Ease out the entrails. Use scissors to snip out anything that remains. With the knife, cut along the vein under the backbone.
3   Wash the cavity under running water.

Peeling and butterflying prawns

Raw prawns can be cooked in or out of their shells; some recipes call for them to be 'butterflied'.

1 To peel prawns, pull off the head and put to one side (it can be used later for making stock). Using pointed scissors, cut through the soft shell on the belly side.

2 Prise the shell off, leaving the tail attached. (Put the shell to one side, with the head.)

3 Using a small sharp knife, make a shallow cut along the length of the back of the prawn.

4 Using the point of the knife, carefully remove and discard the black vein (the intestinal tract) that runs along the back of the prawn.

5 To 'butterfly' the prawn, cut halfway through the flesh lengthways from the head end to the base of the tail, and open up the prawn.

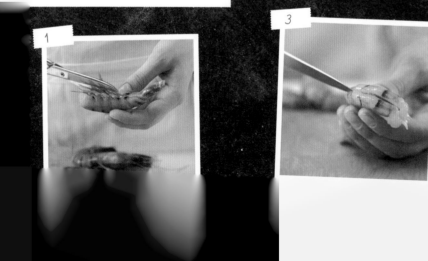

Saffron and Lime Prawns

Hands-on time: 10 minutes, plus marinating
Cooking time: 4 minutes

finely grated zest and juice of 1 lime
a large pinch of saffron
1 garlic clove, crushed
2 small red chillies, seeded and very
   finely chopped (see Safety Tip)
75ml (3fl oz) extra virgin olive oil
32 raw tiger prawns, peeled and
   deveined (see page 51)
salad and pitta bread or griddled
   garlic bread to serve

1 Put the lime zest and juice into a
small pan and heat gently. Add
the saffron and leave to soak for
5 minutes. Stir in the garlic and
chillies and add the oil. Pour into
a screw-topped jar, secure the lid
tightly and shake well.
2 Put the prawns into a shallow dish,
add the marinade, cover and leave
for at least 1 hour.
3 Preheat the barbecue or grill. Soak
eight bamboo skewers in water for
20 minutes.

4 Thread four prawns on to each
skewer. Lay the skewers on the
barbecue or grill and cook for about
2 minutes on each side until they've
just turned pink. Serve immediately,
with salad and warm pitta bread or
griddled garlic bread.

SAFETY TIP

Chillies can be quite mild to
blisteringly hot, depending on
the type of chilli and its ripeness.
Taste a small piece first to
check it's not too hot for you. Be
extremely careful when handling
chillies not to touch or rub your
eyes with your fingers, or they will
sting. Wash knives immediately
after handling chillies. As a
precaution, use rubber gloves
when preparing them, if you like.

Serves 8

Steam-grilled Oriental Salmon

Hands-on time: 15 minutes
Cooking time: 10 minutes

sesame oil to grease
4 salmon fillets, about 150g (5oz) each
   and 2.5cm (1in) thick
4 tbsp soy sauce
200g (7oz) pak choi or spinach
2.5cm (1in) piece fresh root ginger,
   peeled and coarsely grated
4 spring onions, sliced
fresh coriander sprigs to garnish
fragrant Thai rice to serve

1 Preheat the barbecue or grill. Lightly grease four large sheets of foil, each about 35.5cm (14in) square, with sesame oil. Put a salmon fillet in the centre of each piece of foil and drizzle with 1 tbsp soy sauce.

2 Divide the pak choi or spinach leaves, ginger and spring onions among the salmon fillets, then fold up the foil loosely but neatly to form parcels. Seal the edges well so that the parcels can be turned over during cooking; make sure the foil parcels are large enough to allow for the expansion of air that takes place as the salmon begins to cook.

3 Put the parcels on the barbecue or under a hot grill and cook for 4-5 minutes on each side. Serve the sealed parcels to your guests at the table – warn them to watch out as they open the parcels, though, as the steam builds up inside. Garnish with coriander sprigs and serve with fragrant Thai rice.

Serves 4

Lemon Tuna

Hands-on time: 15–20 minutes, plus marinating
Cooking time: about 6 minutes

3 large lemons
2 garlic cloves, crushed
100ml (3½fl oz) extra virgin olive oil
900g (2lb) fresh tuna in one piece
3 tbsp freshly chopped
    flat-leafed parsley
freshly ground black pepper
flatbread to serve

1 Finely grate the zest from one lemon
   and squeeze the juice from the
   grated lemon and one other lemon.
   Mix the zest and juice with the
   garlic and oil and season well with
   ground black pepper.

2 Cut the tuna in half lengthways,
   then cut into strips about 2cm (¾in)
   thick. Lay the strips in a shallow
   dish, pour the marinade over, then
   turn the fish to coat. Cover and leave
   for at least 30 minutes and up to
   1 hour.

3 Preheat the barbecue or grill. Soak
   eight bamboo skewers in water for
   20 minutes.

4 Fold the strips of tuna and thread on
   to the skewers. Cut the remaining
   lemon into eight wedges and push
   one on to each skewer. Drizzle
   with any remaining marinade and
   sprinkle the chopped parsley along
   each skewer.

5 Lay the skewers on the barbecue
   or under a hot grill and cook for
   2–3 minutes on each side. Serve
   immediately with warmed flatbread.

Serves 8

Sardines with Mediterranean Vegetables

Hands-on time: 15 minutes
Cooking time: 20 minutes

3 tbsp olive oil, plus extra to drizzle
2 red onions, about 300g (11oz), peeled, halved and cut into petals
2 garlic cloves, crushed
2 red peppers, about 375g (13oz), halved, seeded and cut into chunks
225g (8oz) courgettes, cut into small chunks
900g (2lb) sardines (about 16), cleaned
lemon juice to drizzle
salt and freshly ground black pepper
small fresh basil sprigs to garnish

1 Heat the oil in a large griddle pan or preheat the grill. Add the onions and fry for 2–3 minutes until almost soft. Add the garlic and peppers and stir-fry for 5 minutes, then add the courgettes and stir-fry for 4–5 minutes until almost soft. Remove from the griddle and keep warm.

2 Season the sardines and cook on the griddle or under a hot grill for 3–4 minutes on each side until cooked in the centre.

3 Drizzle the sardines with a little oil and lemon juice. Garnish with basil sprigs and serve with the vegetables.

SAVE TIME

Complete the recipe to the end of step 1, then cover and chill for up to 3 hours.
When ready to serve, stir-fry the vegetables for 2–3 minutes until hot and complete the recipe.

Serves 4

Perfect Poultry

Chicken is a popular and versatile choice for the barbecue; it lends itself to a huge range of flavourings, marinades and sauces and can be cooked in a variety of ways. Always follow correct food hygiene when handling raw poultry (see page 47).

Spatchcocking

A technique to flatten smaller poultry and guinea fowl for grilling or cooking on the barbecue.

1 Hold the bird on a board, breast down. Cut through one side of the backbone with poultry shears. Repeat on the other side and remove the backbone.
2 Turn the bird over, then press down until you hear the breastbone crack.
3 Thread skewers through the legs and breasts.

Cooking chicken

Grilling is a perfect way to cook pieces of poultry such as breast fillets or strips or chunks threaded on to skewers.

1 Marinate (see page 76) the poultry pieces for at least 30 minutes, drain and pat dry. Alternatively, brush the poultry with a flavoured oil.

2 Put the pieces on a wire rack over a grill pan or roasting tin, and set the pan under a preheated grill so that it is about 7.5cm (3in) from the heat source. Alternatively, place directly on an oiled barbecue rack.

3 Every few minutes brush a little of the marinade or a teaspoon of oil over the poultry.

4 When cooked on one side, turn with tongs and cook the other side until cooked through. Avoid piercing the flesh when turning – if the juices run out the cooked flesh may be dry.

Grilling times

Turn the chicken two or three times during cooking.

Kebabs	8–12 minutes
Thighs	10–15 minutes
Breast fillet	10–20 minutes
Spatchcocked bird	20–30 minutes

Safety Tip

Always test that chicken is cooked all the way through, even if it looks cooked on the outside. Test by piercing the thickest part of the meat with a thin skewer: if the juices run clear the meat is cooked through; if not, put back on to the barbecue or grill for a few minutes.

Marinated Poussins

Hands-on time: 30 minutes, plus overnight marinating
Cooking time: 30 minutes

150ml (¼ pint) bourbon
15g (½oz) soft brown sugar
50ml (2fl oz) clear honey
50ml (2fl oz) tomato ketchup
2 tbsp wholegrain mustard
1 tbsp white wine vinegar
3 garlic cloves, crushed
1 tsp each salt and freshly ground
    black pepper
4 poussins
chargrilled peppers, tomatoes and
    onions garnished with flat-leafed
    parsley to serve

1 Mix the bourbon, sugar, honey, tomato ketchup and mustard together. Stir in the vinegar, garlic, salt and ground black pepper.

2 Put the poussins breast down on a chopping board, then cut through either side of the backbone with poultry shears or a pair of strong sharp scissors and remove it. Open out the poussins, cover them with clingfilm and flatten them slightly by tapping them with the base of a heavy pan. Put the poussins in a shallow glass dish and pour the bourbon marinade over the top, then cover and chill overnight.

3 Preheat the barbecue or grill. Soak eight wooden skewers in water for 20 minutes. Thread the skewers through the legs and breasts of the poussins, keeping the marinade to one side. Cook the poussins for 30 minutes or until cooked through, basting from time to time with the reserved marinade. Serve with the peppers, tomatoes and onions.

Serves 4

Garlic and Thyme Chicken

TAKE 5

Hands-on time: 10 minutes
Cooking time: about 15 minutes

2 garlic cloves, crushed
2 tbsp freshly chopped thyme leaves
2 tbsp olive oil
4 chicken thighs
salt and freshly ground black pepper

1 Preheat the barbecue or grill. Mix together the garlic, thyme and oil in a large bowl. Season with salt and ground black pepper.

2 Using a sharp knife, make two or three slits in each chicken thigh. Put the chicken into the bowl and toss to coat thoroughly. Grill for 5–7 minutes on each side until golden and cooked through.

SAVE TIME

Marinate the chicken 3 hours in advance and chill.

Sticky Chicken Wings

TAKE 5

🍴 **Hands-on time:** 10 minutes, plus marinating (optional)
Cooking time: about 45 minutes

4 tbsp runny honey
4 tbsp wholegrain mustard
12 large chicken wings
salt and freshly ground black pepper
grilled corn on the cob and green
   salad to serve

SAVE EFFORT

An easy way to get a brand new dish
is to try different marinades:
**Hoisin, Sesame and Orange
Marinade**: mix together 6 tbsp hoisin
sauce, 1 tbsp sesame seeds and the
juice of ½ orange. Add the chicken
wings and toss to coat.
Middle Eastern Marinade: mix
together 3 tbsp harissa paste, 1 tbsp
tomato purée and 3 tbsp olive oil. Stir
in a small handful each of freshly
chopped mint and parsley, add the
chicken wings and toss to coat.

1 Put the honey and mustard into a
large glass dish and mix together.
Add the chicken wings and toss
to coat. Season well with salt
and ground black pepper. Cook
immediately or, if you've time, cover
and chill marinate for about 2 hours.

2 Preheat the barbecue or grill. Lift
the wings from the marinade and
cook for 8–10 minutes on each side
until cooked through. Alternatively,
roast in a preheated oven, 200°C
(180°C fan oven) mark 6, for 40–45
minutes. Serve hot, with grilled corn
on the cob and a green salad.

Serves 4

Fiery Mango Chicken

Hands-on time: 15 minutes, plus marinating
Cooking time: 10 minutes

4 tbsp hot mango chutney (or ordinary mango chutney, plus ½ tsp Tabasco)
grated zest and juice of 1 lime
4 tbsp natural yogurt
2 tbsp freshly chopped coriander
1 small green chilli (optional), seeded and finely chopped (see Safety Tip, page 52)
4 chicken breasts with skin on
1 large ripe mango, peeled and stoned
oil to brush
salt and freshly ground black pepper
fresh coriander sprigs and lime wedges to garnish

1 Mix together the chutney, lime zest and juice, yogurt, chopped coriander and, if you like it spicy, the chilli.

2 Put the chicken breasts, skin side down, on the worksurface, cover with clingfilm and lightly beat with a rolling pin. Slice each into three pieces and put into the yogurt mixture, then stir to coat. Cover and chill for at least 30 minutes or overnight.

3 Preheat the barbecue or grill. Slice the mango into four thick pieces. Brush lightly with oil and season well with salt and ground black pepper. Barbecue or grill for about 2 minutes on each side – the fruit should be lightly charred but still firm. Put to one side.

4 Barbecue or grill the chicken for 3–5 minutes on each side until golden. Serve with the grilled mango, garnished with coriander sprigs and lime wedges.

SAVE TIME

Marinate the chicken the night before you plan to cook.

Serves 4

Perfect Meat

Sizzling sausages, succulent lamb chops or juicy steaks are often the highlight of the barbecue. These tips will ensure your meat is cooked the way you like it. Always follow correct food hygiene when handling raw meat (see page 47).

Tenderising

Some cuts of steak benefit from tenderising before you grill them. There are two ways to do it: by pounding or scoring.

1 **Pounding** Lay the steaks in a single layer on a large piece of clingfilm or waxed paper. Lay another sheet on top of the slices and pound gently with a rolling pin, small frying pan or the flat side of a meat mallet.

2 **Scoring** This is useful for cuts that have long, tough fibres, such as flank. It allows a marinade to penetrate more deeply. Lay the steak on the chopping board and, using a long, very sharp knife, make shallow cuts in one direction across the surface. Make another set of cuts at a 45-degree angle to the first. Now turn the meat over and repeat on the other side.

Perfect griddled meat

- Get the griddle smoking hot before putting on the meat.
- You may find that you can cook without oil as long as you let the meat sear thoroughly before turning.
- Put the meat on the griddle and leave for about half the time suggested in the chart (below). When it is cooked it will be easy to turn, so if it seems to be sticking leave for another 30 seconds–1 minute.

Boiling sausages before you barbecue them saves cooking time and reduces the risk of burning on the barbecue.
Put the sausages in a pan of boiling water, bring back to the boil and simmer gently for 3 minutes, then drain and leave to cool completely. Barbecue for 7–8 minutes..

Grilling times

These cooking guidelines are useful whether you are cooking meat on the barbecue, a griddle or under a hot grill. These are total cooking times; turn the meat once during cooking. Timings are approximate, for a piece of meat 2.5cm (1in) thick.

Cut	Rare	Medium	Well done
Beef fillet	3–5 minutes	6–7 minutes	8–10 minutes
Other beef steaks	5–6 minutes	8–12 minutes	15–18 minutes
Lamb chops/steaks	8–10 minutes	10–14 minutes	
Lamb cutlets	6–10 minutes	8–12 minutes	
Boned leg of lamb	35–40 minutes	45–50 minutes	
Pork chops/steaks	8–10 minutes	10–14 minutes	
Sausages (see Save Time)	10–15 minutes		

Teriyaki Beef Sandwiches

Hands-on time: 25 minutes, plus marinating
Cooking time: about 25 minutes, plus resting

700g (1½lb) piece beef sirloin or rump
  steak, thickly sliced
6 tbsp teriyaki marinade
1 tbsp sesame oil
300ml (½ pint) mayonnaise
4 tsp wasabi paste (see Save Effort)
2 ciabatta loaves, split in half
  lengthways
250g (9oz) baby plum tomatoes,
  threaded on to metal skewers
olive oil to brush
75g (3oz) fresh rocket
1 small radicchio, shredded
salt and freshly ground black pepper

1 Trim any fat or sinew from the beef
  and place it in a single layer in a
  shallow glass dish. Mix together
  the teriyaki marinade and sesame
  oil and pour over the meat, turning
  so that it's evenly coated. Cover
  and leave in the fridge for at least
  4 hours or overnight, turning
  occasionally.

2 Mix the mayonnaise with the
  wasabi, season with salt and ground
  black pepper, then cover and leave
  in a cool place.

3 Preheat the barbecue or grill.
  Remove the meat from the marinade
  and pat dry with kitchen paper.
  Cook for 15–20 minutes for medium
  rare and 20–25 minutes for well
  done, turning frequently to ensure
  even cooking. Transfer to a board,
  cover with foil and leave to rest for
  10 minutes.

4 Meanwhile, toast the ciabatta halves
  on the barbecue or grill, wrap in foil
  and put to one side on the barbecue
  to keep warm. Brush the tomato

SAVE EFFORT

Wasabi paste is a Japanese
condiment, green in colour and
extremely hot – a little goes a long
way. If you can't get it, use creamed
horseradish instead.

Serves 6

skewers with a little olive oil and cook for 1–2 minutes on each side.

5 Slice the beef thinly. Spread two halves of ciabatta liberally with the mayonnaise mixture, top each with rocket and radicchio, slices

of warm beef and the tomatoes. Finally, top with more mayonnaise and sandwich together with the remaining ciabatta halves. Cut each loaf into three before serving.

Barbecued Lamb Steaks

Hands-on time: 15 minutes, plus marinating
Cooking time: about 12 minutes

a small bunch each of fresh flat-leafed
   parsley and fresh mint (or any other
   herbs), roughly chopped
3 garlic cloves, sliced
1 tbsp Dijon or wholegrain mustard
juice of 2 small lemons
4 tbsp olive oil
4 thick lamb leg steaks
lemon wedges, rocket and crusty
   bread or couscous to serve

SAVE TIME

Marinate the lamb for up to 1 hour
before you plan to cook.

1 Put the herbs into a small bowl. Add
   the garlic, mustard, lemon juice and
   oil and mix well. Put the lamb into
   a glass dish and spoon the herb
   mixture over it. Cover the dish and
   marinate for at least 10 minutes.
2 Preheat the barbecue or griddle.
   Cook the lamb steaks for about
   4 minutes on each side (or 5–6
   minutes if you like them well done)
   until golden and crusted. Serve
   hot, with lemon wedges, rocket and
   bread or couscous.

Serves 4

Take 5 Super Marinades

Quick and Easy
Combine olive oil, lemon or lime juice and chopped garlic, pour over vegetables, fish or shellfish, chicken or meat and marinate in the fridge for at least 1 hour.

Lemon and Rosemary
Mix together the coarsely grated zest and juice of 1 lemon with 2 tbsp roughly chopped fresh rosemary and 6 tbsp olive oil. Use for vegetables, fish, chicken or lamb.

Spicy Tomato
Mix together 8 tbsp tomato ketchup with 2 tbsp soy sauce, 2 tbsp chilli sauce and 4 tbsp red wine. Add 2 tsp Jamaican jerk seasoning. Use for chicken, pork or sausages.

Pineapple and Coconut
Blend ¼ peeled chopped pineapple with the scooped-out flesh of ½ lime until smooth. Add 200ml (7fl oz) coconut milk and 1 tsp Tabasco sauce. Use for chicken or pork.

Hot and Spicy
Combine 1 crushed garlic clove, 2 tbsp ground coriander, 2 tbsp ground cumin, 1 tbsp paprika, 1 seeded and chopped red chilli (see Safety Tip, page 52), the juice of ½ lemon, 2 tbsp soy sauce and 8 thyme sprigs. Use for chicken, pork or lamb.

SAVE TIME
One of the best ways to get ahead when barbecuing or grilling food is to marinate it overnight so that the flavour of the marinade has time to permeate the food. If you're in a rush, you should allow at least 30 minutes–1 hour for the marinade to flavour the food.

Take 5 Top Tips

Top tips

- Use a large, sealable plastic bag when marinating food: it coats the food more easily, cuts down on washing up, and takes up less space in the fridge than a bowl.
- Marinades will not penetrate poultry skin, so remove the skin or cut slashes in it before mixing the poultry with the marinade.
- Use just enough marinade to coat poultry or meat generously: it is wasteful to use too much, as most will be left in the bottom of the container. It cannot be reused once it has been in contact with raw flesh.
- Dry marinated meat to remove liquid from the surface before cooking. Shake off excess marinade and pat dry with kitchen paper.
- Pay attention when using marinades or sweet glazes made with sugar or honey, as they tend to burn if not watched carefully.

Spice rubs

Sometimes referred to as a dry marinade, spice rubs are a great way to add flavour to meat and poultry. They don't penetrate far into the flesh, but give an excellent flavour on and just under the crust. Make them with crushed garlic, dried herbs or spices, and plenty of ground black pepper. Rub into the meat and marinate for at least 30 minutes or up to 8 hours.

Flavoured Oils

Flavoured oils – look for lemon, garlic, basil and chilli flavours – can be used as a marinade. Alternatively, just brush the oil over the food before you grill it.

Save Time

Ready-made tikka and teriyaki marinades are perfect for most kinds of poultry and meat as well as 'meaty' fish such as tuna.

Lamb with Tapenade

Hands-on time: 5 minutes, plus marinating
Cooking time: about 10 minutes

6 tbsp olive oil
4 tbsp ready-made tapenade
2 tbsp Pernod or Ricard
2 garlic cloves, crushed
8 loin lamb chops, each about
125g (4oz)
freshly ground black pepper
grilled sliced fennel and courgettes
and lemon halves to serve

1 Mix together the oil, tapenade, Pernod or Ricard and the garlic, then rub into the lamb chops and season with ground black pepper. Leave to marinate for at least 30 minutes or overnight.

2 Preheat the barbecue or griddle. Cook the chops for 4–5 minutes on each side. Serve with lightly grilled fennel slices and courgettes and some lemon halves to squeeze over.

SAVE EFFORT

The marinade is ideal for other cuts of lamb, such as steaks or fillets, or spread over a boned shoulder or leg.

Serves 4

Chinese Spare Ribs

TAKE
5

🍴 **Hands-on time:** 5 minutes, plus marinating (optional)
Cooking time: about 45 minutes

10 tbsp hoisin sauce
3 tbsp tomato ketchup
1 garlic clove, crushed
2 × 10-bone baby rack of ribs
(available from butchers), cut
into individual ribs
salt and freshly ground black pepper

1 Put the hoisin sauce, ketchup and
garlic into a large shallow dish.
Season with salt and ground black
pepper and stir everything together
until combined.

2 Add the ribs and toss to coat,
spooning the marinade over to
cover completely. You can either
cook the ribs immediately or, if you
have time, cover and chill them for
2 hours or overnight.

3 Preheat the barbecue or grill until
medium-hot. Alternatively, preheat
the oven to 200°C (180°C fan
oven) mark 6. Lift the ribs from the
marinade and barbecue or grill for
10–12 minutes on each side, or roast
in the oven for 45 minutes.

SAVE TIME

Marinate the ribs the night before
you plan to cook.

Serves 4

Potato and Sausage Skewers

Hands-on time: 15 minutes
Cooking time: 18 minutes

36 even-size new potatoes
6 tbsp olive oil, plus extra to brush
12 thick sausages
2 tbsp freshly chopped mint
50g (2oz) freshly grated Parmesan
salt and freshly ground black pepper
rocket to serve

1 Preheat the barbecue. Soak twelve wooden skewers in water for 20 minutes. Boil the potatoes in salted water for about 10 minutes until almost tender. Drain well and toss with the oil, then season with salt and ground black pepper.

2 Cut each sausage into three and thread on to the skewers alternately with the potatoes. Brush with oil and barbecue for about 8 minutes, turning from time to time, until the sausages are cooked through and the potatoes begin to char.

3 Meanwhile, put the mint into a bowl, add the Parmesan and stir together until well mixed.

4 When the sausages are cooked, remove the skewers from the barbecue and, while still hot, sprinkle with the mint and Parmesan mixture. Serve with rocket.

Serves 6

BBQ-perfect Veg

Garlic, chillies and tomatoes are key flavouring ingredients of many barbecue dishes. It's worth bearing in mind that vegetables also have a lovely flavour when cooked on the griddle as well as attractive browned lines if you use a ridged griddle.

Corn on the cob

The sugar in corn starts to turn to starch soon after picking so it is best eaten as soon as possible after picking or buying. To bake, microwave or barbecue corn, leave it in its husk. To boil, you will need to remove it from its husk. Corn kernels add a crunchy sweetness to any salad.

1 **To husk** pull away the green papery husks from the ear, a few at a time, until the whole ear is exposed.
2 Grasp the stalk and snap it off, taking all the husks with it. Rub the cob firmly with your hand to remove all the silky threads.
3 **To remove the kernels** hold the ear upright in a large bowl, with the stalk sitting on the base of the bowl. Using a thin-bladed knife, cut off the kernels from top to bottom, turning the cob until they are all removed.

Vegetables to throw on the barbecue

Asparagus Snap off the woody end of the stem; brush with oil and grill over medium-hot coals for 6–8 minutes until just tender.

Aubergines Slice, brush with oil and grill over medium-hot coals for 10–15 minutes, turning once or twice, until tender. Alternatively, cut into chunks and thread on to skewers.

Courgettes Slice, brush with oil and grill over medium-hot coals for 8–10 minutes, turning once, until tender. Alternatively, cut into chunks and thread on to skewers.

Mushrooms Thread on to skewers, brush with oil and grill over medium-hot coals for 5–6 minutes.

Onions Thread baby onions on to skewers and grill over medium-hot coals for 10–15 minutes.
Cut larger onions into wedges, thread on to skewers, brush with oil and grill over very hot coals for 30–35 minutes.

Peppers Cut into chunks, brush with oil and grill over medium-hot coals for 8–10 minutes.

Tomatoes Thread small whole tomatoes or cherry tomatoes on to a skewer and grill over medium-hot coals for about 1 minute until the skins begin to blister and burst. Larger tomatoes can be halved, sprinkled with finely chopped garlic, salt and ground black pepper and cooked under a hot grill for 6–8 minutes until tender.

Mediterranean Kebabs

Hands-on time: 15 minutes
Cooking time: about 10 minutes

1 large courgette, cut into chunks
1 red pepper, seeded and cut
  into chunks
12 cherry tomatoes
125g (4oz) halloumi cheese, cubed
100g (3½oz) natural yogurt
1 tsp ground cumin
2 tbsp olive oil
a squeeze of lemon
1 lemon, cut into eight wedges
couscous tossed with freshly chopped
  flat-leafed parsley to serve

1 Preheat the barbecue or grill. Soak eight wooden skewers in water for 20 minutes. Put the courgette into a large bowl with the red pepper, tomatoes and halloumi cheese. Add the yogurt, cumin, oil and a squeeze of lemon and mix.

2 Push a lemon wedge on to each skewer, then divide the vegetables and cheese among the skewers. Grill the kebabs, turning regularly, for 8–10 minutes until the vegetables are tender and the halloumi is nicely charred. Serve with couscous.

Serves 4

Aubergine, Feta and Tomato Stacks

Hands-on time: 10 minutes
Cooking time: 12 minutes

200g (7oz) feta, crumbled
2 tbsp olive oil, plus extra to brush
1 garlic clove, crushed, plus 1 garlic clove to rub
2 plump aubergines, cut into 1cm (½in) thick slices
a handful of fresh basil leaves, torn
3 large vine-ripened tomatoes, each sliced into four
salt and freshly ground black pepper
cocktail sticks
rocket and toasted ciabatta to serve

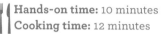

SAVE EFFORT

For an easy way to get a brand new dish, replace the feta with sliced mozzarella, or smoked mozzarella. Mix some olive oil with the crushed garlic, brush over the mozzarella and stack up in step 3.

1 Preheat the barbecue or grill. Put the feta into a bowl, stir in the oil and garlic, season with salt and ground black pepper and put to one side.

2 Brush each aubergine slice with a little oil and barbecue or grill for about 6 minutes, turning occasionally until softened and golden. Take off the heat.

3 Sprinkle a little of the feta mixture on to six of the aubergine slices, put some torn basil leaves on top, then a slice of tomato. Season well. Repeat with the feta mixture, basil leaves, aubergine and tomato. Finish with an aubergine slice and press down firmly.

4 Secure each stack with a cocktail stick. Either use a well-oiled hinged grill rack, or wrap the stacks in foil and barbecue or grill for 2–3 minutes on each side. Serve with rocket leaves and toasted ciabatta rubbed with a garlic clove.

Serves 6

Red Onions with Rosemary Dressing

Hands-on time: 20 minutes
Cooking time: about 35 minutes

3 large red onions, root intact, each cut into eight wedges
6 tbsp olive oil
4 tbsp balsamic vinegar
2 tsp freshly chopped rosemary
salt and freshly ground black pepper

1 Preheat the barbecue. Soak eight wooden skewers in water for 20 minutes. Thread the onion wedges on to the skewers. Brush with about 3 tbsp oil, then season well with salt and ground black pepper.

2 Barbecue the onion kebabs for 30–35 minutes, turning from time to time and brushing with oil when necessary, until they are tender and lightly charred.

3 To make the dressing, mix the balsamic vinegar with the remaining olive oil and the rosemary. Drizzle the rosemary dressing over the cooked onions and serve.

SAVE TIME

Make the dressing several hours ahead. Mix well before using.

Serves 8

Ultimate Burgers

Classic Hamburger

Hands-on time: 20 minutes, plus chilling
Cooking time: 10 minutes

1kg (2¼lb) extra-lean minced beef
2 tsp salt
2 tbsp steak seasoning
sunflower oil to brush
6 large soft rolls, halved
6 thin-cut slices havarti or
   raclette cheese
4 small cocktail gherkins, sliced
   lengthways
6 tbsp mustard mayonnaise
6 lettuce leaves, such as frisée
4 large vine-ripened tomatoes,
   thickly sliced
2 large shallots, sliced into thin rings
freshly ground black pepper

1 Put the minced beef into a large bowl and add the salt, steak seasoning and plenty of ground black pepper. Use your hands to mix the ingredients together thoroughly. Lightly oil the inside of six 10cm (4in) rosti rings and put on a foil-lined baking sheet. Press the meat firmly into the rings, or use your hands to shape the mixture into six even-size patties. Cover with clingfilm and chill for at least 1 hour.

2 Heat a large griddle pan until it's really hot. Put the rolls, cut sides down, on the griddle and toast. Remove from the pan.

3 Lightly oil the griddle, ease the burgers out of the moulds and brush with oil. Griddle over a medium heat for about 3 minutes, then turn the burgers over carefully. Put a slice of cheese and a few slices of gherkin on top of each and cook for 3 minutes more.

Serves 6

4 While the burgers are cooking, spread the mayonnaise on the toasted side of the rolls. Add the lettuce, tomatoes and shallots. Put the burgers on top and sandwich with the other half-rolls.

SAVE EFFORT

For an easy way to make this into a more sophisticated burger, replace the cheese and gherkins with thick slices of ripe avocado and use a generous handful of fresh rocket instead of the lettuce.

The Ultimate Cheeseburger

Hands-on time: 20 minutes, plus chilling (optional)
Cooking time: about 20 minutes

For the burgers

500g (1lb 2oz) steak mince
½ small onion, finely chopped
1 medium egg
½ tbsp Dijon mustard
100g (3½oz) fresh white breadcrumbs
2 tbsp sunflower oil
8 Cheddar slices
salt and freshly ground black pepper

To serve

4 sesame burger buns
Gem lettuce leaves, tomato slices and
  gherkin spears (optional)

1 Put the mince into a large bowl and mix in the onion, egg, mustard, breadcrumbs and plenty of seasoning. Divide the mixture equally into four and shape each portion into a flattened patty. Arrange on a plate, then cover and chill in the fridge for 30 minutes, if you have time.

2 Preheat the oven to 200°C (180°C fan oven) mark 6. Heat the oil in a large frying pan over a medium-high heat and fry the burgers for 8 minutes, turning once, or until each side is well browned. Arrange the burgers on a baking tray and lay a slice of cheese on top of each one. Put into the oven and cook for 6 minutes, then add another slice of cheese and cook for 6 minutes more.

3 Meanwhile, toast the buns. Check to make sure the burgers are cooked through and serve in the buns, topped with lettuce leaves, tomato and gherkin slices, if you like. Great with chips and a crisp green salad.

The Ultimate Barbecue Sauce

To make 300ml (½ pint), you
will need:
3 tbsp olive oil, 3 finely chopped
garlic cloves, 3 tbsp balsamic vinegar,
4 tbsp dry sherry, 3 tbsp sun-dried
tomato paste or tomato purée, 3 tbsp
sweet chilli sauce, 300ml (½ pint)
passata, 5 tbsp runny honey.

1 Put the oil, garlic, vinegar, sherry,
   tomato paste or purée and the
   chilli sauce into a bowl and mix
   well. Pour into a pan, then add
   the passata and honey. Bring to
   the boil, then reduce the heat and
   simmer for 10–15 minutes until thick.

Avocado Salsa

To serve four to six, you will need:
3 large ripe tomatoes, 1 large red
pepper, 2 small red chillies, 1 finely
chopped red onion, 4 tbsp freshly
chopped coriander, 2 tbsp freshly
chopped parsley, 2 ripe avocados, salt
and freshly ground black pepper.

1 Quarter, seed and dice the
   tomatoes. Core, seed and finely
   chop the pepper. Halve, seed and
   finely chop the chillies (see Safety
   Tip, page 52) and combine with
   the tomatoes, peppers, onion and
   herbs.
2 Halve, stone, peel and dice the
   avocados. Add to the salsa and
   season well with salt and ground
   black pepper. Toss well and serve
   within about 10 minutes. (Cut
   avocado flesh will discolour if left
   for longer than this.)

Flavoured butter

A pat of flavoured butter makes an
instant sauce for simply grilled fish,
chicken, meat or vegetables. You
will need:
25g (1oz) soft unsalted butter per
serving, plus flavouring.

1 Beat the softened butter together
   with the flavouring. Turn out on to
   clingfilm, shape into a log and wrap
   tightly.

2 Chill in the fridge for at least 1 hour. Keep for up to one week (or freeze for up to one month).

Flavourings:

For 125g (4oz) unsalted butter.
Anchovy butter: 6 mashed anchovy fillets.
Herb butter: 2 tbsp finely chopped herbs, a squeeze of lemon juice.
Garlic butter: 1 crushed garlic clove, 2 tsp finely chopped fresh parsley.

Salsa verde

This piquant sauce is good for grilled fish and meat. To serve four, you will need:
a small handful of parsley, about 40g (1½oz), 6 tbsp fresh white breadcrumbs, 5 tbsp extra-virgin olive oil, 1 tsp capers, 1 gherkin, 2 tbsp lemon juice, 1 tbsp chopped chives.

1 Put all the ingredients into a food processor. Process until combined.
2 Transfer to a bowl, check the seasoning and adjust as necessary.

Tomato sauce

This contains no oil or butter, so stir some in just before serving. To make 2.5kg (5½lb), you will need:
2.7kg (6lb) ripe tomatoes, 3 finely chopped onions, 6 finely chopped garlic cloves, 150ml (¼ pint) sun-dried tomato paste, 1 tbsp freshly chopped oregano, salt and ground black pepper.

1 Skin, seed and quarter the tomatoes, then chop the flesh.
2 Put all the ingredients in a large pan and bring to the boil. Reduce the heat and simmer, uncovered, over a low heat for 25–30 minutes, stirring occasionally, until the sauce is thick and pulpy. Season to taste, and cook for a few minutes more.
3 Pour into warm, sterilised jars (see page 412). Seal and label, and store in a cool dark place for up to six months.

The All-day Breakfast Burger

Hands-on time: 30 minutes
Cooking time: about 25 minutes

1 tbsp olive oil
150g (5oz) mushrooms, finely chopped
½ small onion, finely chopped
2 tbsp tomato ketchup
1 tbsp Worcestershire sauce
500g (1lb 2oz) pork mince
3 tbsp freshly chopped
  flat-leafed parsley
8 streaky bacon rashers
4 medium eggs
salt and freshly ground black pepper
2 English muffins, halved and toasted,
  to serve

1 Heat the oil in a large frying pan over a high heat and cook the mushrooms for 5 minutes or until tender. Empty into a large bowl and put the pan to one side.

2 Add the onion, tomato ketchup, Worcestershire sauce, pork mince, parsley and plenty of seasoning to the bowl and mix to combine.

3 Divide the mixture equally into four and shape each portion into a flattened patty.

4 Put the pan back on to a medium heat and fry the burgers for 15–18 minutes, turning occasionally, until cooked through.

5 Meanwhile, heat another frying pan and cook the bacon rashers until golden and crisp. Drain on kitchen paper. Crack the eggs into the empty pan and fry them over a gentle heat until the whites are set and the yolks are still soft.

6 Serve each burger on half a toasted muffin, topped with some bacon and a fried egg.

Serves 4

Curried Turkey Burgers

Hands-on time: 25 minutes
Cooking time: about 20 minutes

500g (1lb 2oz) turkey breast mince
2 tbsp medium curry paste
1 shallot, finely chopped
1 garlic clove, crushed
a small handful of fresh parsley,
   chopped, plus extra to garnish
3 tbsp mango chutney
½ tbsp vegetable oil
salt and freshly ground black pepper
Gem lettuce leaves to serve

1 Preheat the oven to 200°C (180°C fan oven) mark 6. Put the turkey mince, curry paste, shallot, garlic and parsley into a large bowl with 1 tbsp of the mango chutney and plenty of seasoning. Mix together until well combined. Divide the mixture equally into four and shape each portion into a flattened patty.

2 Brush the patties with the oil and arrange on a non-stick baking tray. Cook for 15–18 minutes until the burgers are golden brown and cooked through.

3 Serve the burgers and lettuce leaves topped with the remaining mango chutney and some parsley. Top with another lettuce leaf.

HEALTHY TIP

Turkey is the mince to use if you're looking for a healthier burger option.

Make Your Own Mayo

The simplest of accompaniments, mayonnaise goes well with salads, poached fish and poultry. For salads, you can flavour the basic mayonnaise with a variety of herbs, vegetables and fruit.

Mayonnaise

To make about 250ml (9fl oz), you will need:

2 large egg yolks, 1 tsp English mustard, 200ml (7fl oz) sunflower oil, 100ml (3½fl oz) extra virgin olive oil, 1 tsp white wine vinegar or lemon juice, salt and freshly ground black pepper.

1 Put the egg yolks into a 900ml (1½ pint) bowl. Stir in the mustard, 1 tsp salt and plenty of ground black pepper.

2 Combine the oils and add 1 tsp to the egg yolks. Whisk thoroughly, then add another 1 tsp and whisk until thickened. Continue adding about half the oil, 1 tbsp at a time. Whisk in the vinegar or lemon juice, then add the oils in a thin, steady stream until the mayonnaise is thick.

3 Check the seasoning, adding more vinegar or lemon juice if necessary. Cover and chill for up to four days.

2

2

Lemon and Garlic

To make about 150ml (¼ pint), you will need:

175ml (6fl oz) mayonnaise, 1 tbsp grated lemon zest, plus 1 tbsp lemon juice, 2 finely chopped spring onions, 1 garlic clove, crushed, salt and freshly ground black pepper.

1 Put all the ingredients into a medium bowl and beat well to combine. Check the seasoning.
2 Cover and chill for up to two days.

Smoky Pepper

To make about 175ml (6fl oz), you will need:

1 peeled and chopped grilled red pepper, 1 garlic clove, 250ml (9fl oz) mayonnaise, 2 tsp chilli oil, 2 tbsp lemon juice.

1 Put the red pepper, garlic and mayonnaise into a food processor and whiz to combine.
2 Stir in the chilli oil and lemon juice. Cover and chill for up to two days.

Mango

To make about 175ml (6fl oz), you will need:

1 large peeled and stoned mango, 2 tsp freshly chopped coriander, 1 tsp peeled and grated fresh root ginger, juice of 1 lime, 200ml (7fl oz) sunflower oil, salt and freshly ground black pepper.

1 Mash the flesh of the mango in a bowl and add the coriander, ginger and lime juice. Season well with salt and ground black pepper.
2 Slowly whisk in the oil until the mayonnaise is thick. Cover and chill for up to two days.

Italian Burger

Hands-on time: 25 minutes
Cooking time: about 15 minutes

500g (1lb 2oz) beef mince
50g (2oz) sun-dried tomatoes,
  finely chopped
2 tbsp basil pesto
125g (4oz) mozzarella, cut into 4 slices
1 tbsp extra virgin olive oil, plus
  extra to drizzle (optional)
4 ciabatta rolls, split
a large handful of rocket leaves
25g (1oz) pinenuts, toasted
salt and freshly ground black pepper

1 Put the beef, sun-dried tomatoes, pesto and plenty of ground black pepper (the tomatoes will add salt) into a large bowl and stir together. Divide the mixture equally into four. Take one of the meat portions and flatten out into a thin circle on the palm of your hand. Place a mozzarella slice on top and fold the overhanging meat over the cheese, squishing it into a round, flattish patty and fully encasing the cheese. Repeat with the remaining mince mixture and cheese.

2 Heat the oil in a large frying pan over a medium heat and fry the patties for 15 minutes, turning once, or until the burgers are golden brown and cooked through.

3 Toast the ciabatta rolls and serve the burgers in the rolls topped with rocket, pinenuts and a drizzle of oil, if you like.

Serves 4

Honey Mustard Chicken Burger

Hands-on time: 30 minutes, plus chilling (optional)
Cooking time: about 15 minutes

For the burgers

4 skinless chicken breasts,
　roughly chopped
1 tbsp wholegrain mustard
1½ tbsp runny honey
75g (3oz) fresh white breadcrumbs
1 medium egg
finely grated zest of 1 lemon
1 tbsp olive oil
salt and freshly ground black pepper

To serve

3 tbsp mayonnaise
3 tbsp half-fat crème fraîche
½ tbsp lemon juice
½ tbsp wholegrain mustard
4 floury white baps
Gem lettuce leaves (optional)
tomato slices (optional)

1　To make the burgers, whiz the chicken in a food processor until it resembles mince, then empty into a large bowl and mix in the mustard, 1 tbsp of the honey, the breadcrumbs, egg, lemon zest and plenty of seasoning.

2　Divide the mixture equally into four and shape each portion into a flattened patty. Arrange on a plate, then cover and chill for 30 minutes, if you have time.

3　Preheat the oven to 200°C (180°C fan oven) mark 6. Heat the oil in a large pan over a medium-high heat and fry the burgers for 5 minutes, turning occasionally, until each side

SAVE EFFORT

For an easy, delicious variation, replace the chicken breasts with 500g (1lb 2oz) turkey breast mince.

Serves 4

is browned. Arrange the burgers on a baking tray and brush the tops with the remaining honey. Put into the oven and cook for 10–12 minutes more until cooked through.

4 Meanwhile, put the mayonnaise, crème fraîche, lemon juice, mustard and some seasoning into a small bowl and mix together. Put to one side. Halve and toast the baps.

5 Serve the burgers in the toasted baps, topped with lettuce and tomato slices, if you like, with a dollop of the mustard sauce.

Tuna Burger

🍴 **Hands-on time:** 25 minutes
Cooking time: about 15 minutes

3 tbsp toasted sesame oil
1 tbsp vegetable oil
2.5cm (1in) piece fresh root ginger,
   peeled and grated
4 × 125g (4oz) tuna steaks
1 cucumber, ends trimmed
½ tbsp rice wine vinegar
½–1 tbsp red chilli, to taste, seeded
   and finely chopped (see Safety Tip,
   page 52)
½ tbsp sesame seeds
4 slices from a large bloomer loaf
soy sauce to drizzle
salt and freshly ground black pepper

1 Put 1 tbsp of the sesame oil, the
   vegetable oil and ginger into a small
   bowl and stir together. Brush the
   mixture over the tuna steaks and
   put to one side.
2 Peel the cucumber into ribbons with
   a vegetable peeler and put into a
   bowl with the remaining sesame oil,
   the vinegar, chilli, sesame seeds and
   some seasoning. Put to one side.
3 Heat a griddle pan over a high heat
   for a few minutes, then toast the
   bread slices for 2–3 minutes a side
   until toasted with charred lines.
   Divide the toasts among four plates.
4 Add the tuna steaks to the griddle
   pan and cook for 4 minutes, turning
   once, or for longer or shorter
   depending on your preference.
5 Lift the tuna steaks on to the toasts
   and top with the cucumber salad.
   Drizzle with a little soy sauce
   before serving.

Serves 4

Chilli-lime

To make about 100ml (3½fl oz), you will need:

2 tbsp sweet chilli sauce, 1 tbsp freshly chopped coriander, grated zest and juice of 1 lime, 5 tbsp mayonnaise, salt and freshly ground black pepper.

1 Put the chilli sauce into a bowl and stir in the coriander, lime zest and juice and mayonnaise. Check the seasoning.
2 Cover and chill for up to one day.

Coconut

To make 125ml (4fl oz), you will need:

½ quantity Chilli-lime Dressing (see above), 50g (2oz) mayonnaise, 100g (3½oz) Greek-style yogurt, 100ml (3½fl oz) coconut cream.

1 Put all the ingredients into a bowl and, using a balloon whisk, beat everything together until well combined.
2 Cover with clingfilm and chill.

Avocado Crush

Toss 1 large peeled and chopped avocado in 4 tbsp lemon juice. Blend with 100ml (3½fl oz) olive oil and 2 tbsp water. Great with chicken, fish or any salad.

Mustard and Caper

Mash the yolks of 2 hard-boiled eggs with 2 tsp smooth Dijon mustard. Add 2 tbsp white wine vinegar and gradually whisk in 8 tbsp olive oil. Add 2 tbsp chopped capers, 1 tbsp chopped shallot and a pinch of sugar. Season with salt and ground black pepper. Great with barbecued fish, beef, pork or sausages.

Almond and Herb Pesto

Put 50g (2oz) fresh flat-leafed parsley, 1 thick slice stale bread (crust removed), 2 tbsp lemon juice and 1–2 garlic cloves into a food processor and whiz to combine, then whiz in 50g (2oz) toasted almonds and 200ml (7fl oz) olive oil. Great with barbecued vegetables or chicken, or with pasta.

Moroccan Lamb Burger

Hands-on time: 20 minutes
Cooking time: about 20 minutes

For the burgers

1 tsp ground cumin

½ tbsp coriander seeds

1 fat garlic clove

600g (1lb 5oz) lamb mince

finely grated zest of ½ orange

50g (2oz) ready-to-eat dried apricots,
  finely chopped

½ tbsp vegetable oil

salt and freshly ground black pepper

To serve

100g (3½oz) natural yogurt

½–1 tsp harissa paste, to taste

2 tbsp freshly chopped mint

a large handful of watercress

4 flour tortillas or white khobez wraps

1 Pound the cumin, coriander, garlic and plenty of seasoning in a pestle and mortar until fairly smooth. Scrape into a large bowl and stir in the lamb mince, orange zest and apricots. Divide the mixture equally into four and shape each portion into a flattened patty.

2 Heat the oil in a frying pan over a medium heat and cook for 15–18 minutes, turning occasionally, until cooked through.

3 Meanwhile, put the yogurt, harissa, mint and some seasoning into a small bowl and stir together. Serve the burgers and watercress wrapped in the tortillas or wraps, drizzled with harissa sauce.

Serves 4

Mexican Chickpea Burger

Hands-on time: 25 minutes
Cooking time: about 18 minutes

For the burgers

400g can chickpeas, drained
    and rinsed
1 large egg
400g can lentils, drained and rinsed
75g (3oz) fresh white breadcrumbs
4 spring onions, finely sliced
1 green chilli, seeded and finely
    chopped (see Safety Tip, page 52)
finely grated zest of 1 lime
a small handful of fresh coriander,
    roughly chopped
1 tbsp olive oil
salt and freshly ground black pepper

To serve

1 avocado, peeled, stoned and sliced
juice of 1 lime
2 spring onions, finely sliced
2 tomatoes, finely chopped
a small handful of fresh coriander,
    chopped, plus extra to garnish
4 large flour tortilla wraps
soured cream (optional)

1 To make the burgers, put the
  chickpeas, egg and plenty of
  seasoning into a food processor
  and whiz until smooth. Scrape the
  mixture into a large bowl and stir
  in the lentils, breadcrumbs, spring
  onions, chilli, grated lime zest
  and chopped coriander and mix
  to combine. Divide the mixture
  equally into four and shape each
  into a flattened patty.
2 Heat the oil in a large frying pan
  and fry the patties for 10 minutes,
  turning once, or until golden and
  piping hot throughout.

SAVE EFFORT

This is a great way to use
storecupboard chickpeas
and lentils.

Serves 4

3 Meanwhile, put the avocado slices into a bowl and squeeze the juice from half the lime over them. In a separate small bowl, stir together the spring onions, tomatoes, coriander and remaining lime juice.

4 Serve the burgers, avocado and salsa folded into the tortillas, with soured cream, if you like.

Courgette and Anchovy Burgers

Hands-on time: 20 minutes
Cooking time: about 10 minutes

500g (1lb 2oz) courgettes
5 anchovy fillets in oil, finely chopped
50g (2oz) fresh white breadcrumbs
1 medium egg
3 tbsp chopped fresh parsley
1 tbsp wholegrain mustard
plain flour to dust
1 tbsp sunflower oil
4 tbsp natural yogurt
4 tbsp mayonnaise
¼ cucumber, grated
1 tbsp freshly chopped mint
salt and freshly ground black pepper
burger buns, toasted (optional) and
   salad leaves to serve

1 Trim the courgettes, then grate them coarsely. Wrap the grated courgettes in a clean teatowel and squeeze out as much moisture as you can. Put the courgettes into a large bowl, add the anchovies, breadcrumbs, egg, parsley, mustard and some seasoning and mix well. Shape the mixture into four patties and dust them in flour.

2 Heat the oil in a large, non-stick frying pan, add the patties and cook for 8 minutes, carefully turning them once, or until golden brown and piping hot.

3 Meanwhile, mix the yogurt, mayonnaise, cucumber, mint and some seasoning together in a medium bowl. Serve the patties as they are, or in toasted burger buns, if you like, with the yogurt sauce and some salad leaves.

Serves 4

Curried Tofu Burgers

Hands-on time: 20 minutes
Cooking time: about 8 minutes

1 tbsp sunflower oil, plus extra to fry
1 large carrot, finely grated
1 large onion, finely grated
2 tsp coriander seeds, finely crushed
  (optional)
1 garlic clove, crushed
1 tsp curry paste
1 tsp tomato purée
225g pack firm tofu
25g (1oz) fresh wholemeal
  breadcrumbs
25g (1oz) mixed nuts, finely chopped
plain flour to dust
salt and freshly ground black pepper
boiled rice and green vegetables
  to serve

1 Heat the oil in a large frying pan.
Add the carrot and onion and fry for
3–4 minutes until the vegetables are
softened, stirring all the time. Add
the coriander seeds, if you like, the
garlic, curry paste and tomato purée.
Increase the heat and cook for 2
minutes, stirring all the time.

2 Put the tofu into a bowl and mash
with a potato masher. Stir in the
vegetables, breadcrumbs and nuts
and season with salt and ground
black pepper. Beat thoroughly until
the mixture starts to stick together.
With floured hands, shape the
mixture into eight burgers.

3 Heat some oil in a frying pan and
fry the burgers for 3–4 minutes
on each side until golden brown.
Alternatively, brush lightly with oil
and cook under a hot grill for about
3 minutes on each side until golden
brown. Drain on kitchen paper and
serve the burgers hot with boiled
rice and green vegetables.

Picnic on the Beach

Stress-free get-ahead time plan

Up to three days before

- Prepare the syrup for Warming Ginger Soda.

The day before

- Make the Sweetcorn and Bacon Chowder (but don't add the parsley).
- Make the Speedy Cheese Straws.
- Make the Sticky Toffee Pudding.
- Prepare the Mexican Hot Chocolate.
- Prepare the Cheesy Spinach Muffins.
- Prepare the Roasted Pepper and Pea Salads.

On the day, to serve lunch at 2pm

11am
- Make the Fish and Chip Pie.

1.15pm
- Finish the Roasted Pepper Salad. Make and serve the Mexican Hot Chocolate.

1.45pm
- Reheat the chowder and cheese straws. Dilute the ginger soda.

2pm
- Reheat the fish pie, if needed. Serve the chowder and cheese straws with the ginger soda.

2.20pm
- Finish the Pea Salad. Serve the main course.
- Finish off the pudding when you're ready and serve.

Picnic Menu for 6

Mexican Hot Chocolate
Warming Ginger Soda
*

Sweetcorn and Bacon Chowder
with Speedy Cheese Straws
*

Fish and Chip Pie
Cheesy Spinach Muffins
Roasted Pepper Salad
Pea Salad
*

Sticky Toffee Pudding

Mexican Hot Chocolate

Hands-on time: 5 minutes
Cooking time: 15 minutes

1 litre (1¾ pints) semi-skimmed milk
75g (3oz) cocoa powder
75g (3oz) caster sugar
½–1 tsp ground cinnamon
2 large pinches of cayenne pepper
whipped cream and mini
   marshmallows to serve

SAVE TIME

Prepare the hot chocolate to the end
of step 2 up to one day ahead. Cool,
cover and chill. Reheat in a pan as
necessary.

1 Gently heat the milk until nearly
boiling. Put the cocoa powder, sugar,
ground cinnamon and cayenne
pepper into a bowl and mix well.
2 Add a little of the hot milk and mix
until smooth, then stir into the pan
to reheat.
3 Pour into mugs and top with
whipped cream and mini
marshmallows to serve.

Serves 6

Warming Ginger Soda

Hands-on time: 5 minutes
Cooking time: 15 minutes, plus cooling

300g (11oz) unpeeled fresh root ginger, finely sliced

225g (8oz) caster sugar

6 whole cloves

grated zest and juice of 1½ lemons

1 litre (1¾ pints) soda water

fresh mint leaves to decorate

1 Put the ginger into a pan with the sugar, cloves and lemon zest and juice. Add about 600ml (1 pint) cold water to cover. Heat gently to dissolve the sugar, then increase the heat and simmer for 10 minutes. Strain through a fine sieve into a jug.

2 Leave to cool for 10 minutes, then top up with the soda water. Decorate with fresh mint leaves.

SAVE TIME

Make the syrup up to three days ahead and chill. Add the soda water to serve.

Serves 6; makes about 1.6 litres (2 pints)

Sweetcorn and Bacon Chowder

Hands-on time: 10 minutes
Cooking time: about 20 minutes

1 tbsp olive oil

200g (7oz) smoked bacon lardons

1 large onion, finely chopped

2 celery sticks, chopped

2 large carrots, chopped

¼ tsp ground cinnamon

¼ tsp smoked paprika

1.3 litres (2¼ pints) vegetable stock

2 × 198g cans sweetcorn, drained

250ml (8fl oz) double cream

a large handful of fresh parsley,
  roughly chopped

salt and freshly ground black pepper

breadsticks to serve

1 Heat the oil in a large pan and fry the lardons, chopped vegetables and spices for 5–10 minutes until the vegetables are soft.

2 Pour in the stock and bring to the boil, then reduce the heat and simmer for 5 minutes or until the vegetables are tender. Add the sweetcorn, cream and most of the parsley and simmer for 2–3 minutes more.

3 Check the seasoning and divide the soup among six warmed mugs or bowls. Garnish with the remaining parsley and serve with speedy cheese straws.

SAVE TIME

Prepare the chowder up to one day ahead, omitting the parsley. Leave to cool, then empty into a bowl, cover and chill. To serve, reheat in a pan and complete the recipe.

Serves 6

Speedy Cheese Straws

Hands-on time: 10 minutes
Cooking time: about 20 minutes

375g pack ready-rolled puff pastry
plain flour to dust
40g (1½oz) each Parmesan and
   Cheddar, grated
1 medium egg, beaten
¼ tsp paprika
1 tsp poppy seeds

1 Preheat the oven to 200°C (180°C fan oven) mark 6. Unroll the pastry on to a floured surface. Sprinkle most of the cheese over it, then fold the pastry in half and then in half again. Re-roll the pastry to make a 30.5 × 12.5cm (12 × 5in) rectangle. Trim the edges and discard.

2 Brush with beaten egg, then sprinkle the remaining cheese, the paprika and poppy seeds over the surface. Cut into 2cm (¾in) wide strips across the width of the pastry, then transfer to a baking sheet and cook for 15–20 minutes until deep golden brown. Serve warm or at room temperature.

SAVE TIME

These cheese straws are best when fresh, but can be made up to one day ahead – leave to cool completely and store in an airtight tin. When ready to serve, heat in a preheated 200°C (180°C fan oven) mark 6 oven for about 5 minutes to crisp up.

Makes about 14

Fish and Chip Pie

Hands-on time: 45 minutes, plus chilling
Cooking time: about 1 hour 25 minutes

For the pastry

225g (8oz) plain flour, plus extra
  to dust

150g (5oz) butter, chilled and cut
  into cubes

finely grated zest of 1 lemon

salt and freshly ground black pepper

For the filling

2 medium potatoes, about 300g (11oz),
  unpeeled

1 tbsp olive oil

500g (1lb 2oz) white fish fillets,
  skinned

150g (5oz) cooked king prawns

300ml (½ pint) double cream

2 medium eggs

a small handful of fresh parsley,
  finely chopped

1 To make the pastry, put the flour, butter, lemon zest and some seasoning into a food processor and whiz until the mixture resembles fine breadcrumbs. Alternatively, rub the butter into the flour mixture using your fingers. Add 2 tbsp icy cold water and whiz again (or stir in with a blunt-ended knife) until the pastry just comes together. Tip on to a worksurface and bring together using your hands. Wrap in clingfilm and chill for 30 minutes.

2 Meanwhile, cut the potatoes into 1.5cm (½in) cubes. Heat half the oil in a large, non-stick frying pan and cook the potatoes for 15 minutes, tossing occasionally, or until golden and tender. Empty into a bowl and put to one side with the empty pan.

3 Preheat the oven to 190°C (170°C fan oven) mark 5. Lightly flour a worksurface and roll out the pastry. Use to line a 22 × 4cm (8½ × 1½in) deep-fluted tart tin. Prick the base

Serves 6–8

SAVE TIME

Make the pie up to 3 hours ahead. Carefully remove from the tin and leave to cool to room temperature. To serve warm, gently reheat on a baking tray in a preheated 170°C (150°C fan oven) mark 3 oven for 15 minutes.

all over, then chill for 15 minutes.

4 Put the empty pan back on to the heat and add the remaining oil. Fry the fish for 4 minutes, turning once, or until just cooked. Lift out of the pan and put into a sieve set over a bowl to drain off any liquid.

5 Blind bake the pastry case for 20 minutes, removing the beans and paper for the last 5 minutes of cooking. Reduce the oven temperature to 170°C (150°C fan oven) mark 3.

6 Flake the fish into big pieces and put into the cooked pastry case with the cooked prawns and potatoes. Mix the cream, eggs, parsley and plenty of seasoning in a jug. Pour as much mixture into the pastry case as possible, then cook for about 45 minutes until golden and set. Serve warm or at room temperature.

Cheesy Spinach Muffins

Hands-on time: 15 minutes
Cooking time: about 15 minutes

100g (3½oz) baby spinach
150g (5oz) self-raising flour
1 tsp baking powder
25g (1oz) Parmesan, grated
50g (2oz) Cheddar, finely cubed
25g (1oz) butter, melted
100ml (3½fl oz) milk
2 medium eggs
a small handful of fresh parsley,
   finely chopped
salt and freshly ground black pepper

SAVE TIME

Prepare the muffins to the end of step 2 up to one day ahead. Put the chopped spinach into a bowl, then cover and chill. Cover the flour and cheese mixture and chill, then complete the recipe to serve.

1 Preheat the oven to 200°C (180°C fan oven) mark 6. Line six holes in a 12-hole muffin tin with paper muffin cases. Put the spinach into a sieve and pour boiling water from the kettle over it until it wilts. Leave the spinach to cool, then squeeze out as much water as you can before finely chopping it. Put to one side.

2 Put the flour, baking powder, most of the Parmesan and Cheddar and some seasoning into a bowl and mix well.

3 In a separate jug, whisk together the butter, milk, eggs, parsley and chopped spinach. Quickly mix the wet ingredients into the dry. Don't worry if there are floury lumps, as these will cook out.

4 Divide the mixture evenly among the paper cases, then sprinkle the remaining cheeses on top. Cook for 12–15 minutes until the muffins are risen, golden and cooked through. Serve warm.

Makes 6

Roasted Pepper Salad

Hands-on time: 20 minutes
Cooking time: about 20 minutes

6 mixed peppers
1 tbsp balsamic vinegar
2 tbsp olive oil
1 tbsp runny honey
½ tbsp capers, rinsed and
  finely chopped
salt and freshly ground black pepper
2 tbsp flaked almonds, toasted,
  to garnish

SAVE TIME

Prepare the salad to the end of
step 2 up to one day ahead. Chill
the peppers. Cover and chill the
dressing. Complete the recipe up
to 1 hour before serving.
If you're short on time, use ready-
roasted peppers.

1 Preheat the grill to high and set a
  rack about 15cm (6in) away from
  the heat source. Put the peppers on
  a baking sheet and grill for 15–20
  minutes, turning frequently, until
  the skin is blistered and black.
  Transfer the peppers to a large bowl,
  cover tightly with clingfilm and
  leave to cool.

2 Meanwhile, put the vinegar, oil,
  honey, capers and some seasoning
  into a small jug and mix well. When
  the peppers are cool, peel off and
  discard the blackened skins. Seed
  and cut into thick strips.

3 Put the peppers into a serving dish
  and toss the dressing through.
  Garnish with the almonds and serve
  as a side dish.

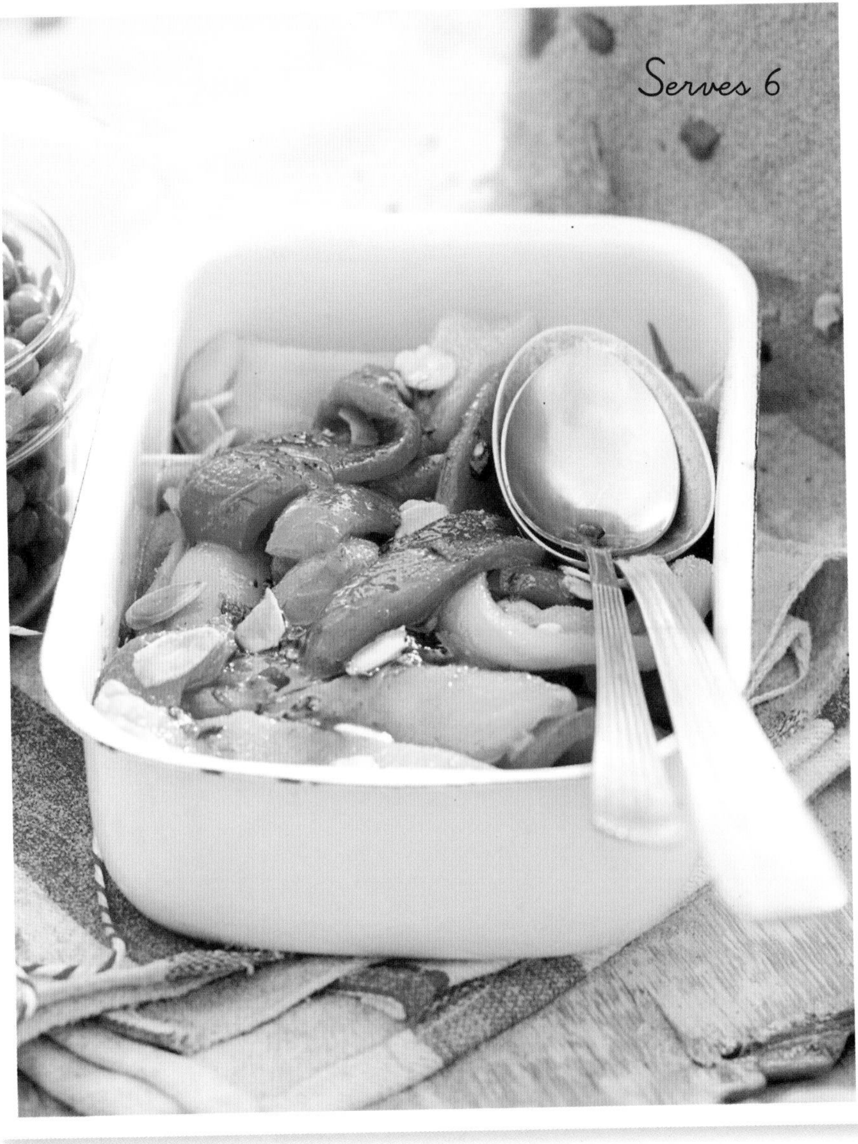

Serves 6

Pea Salad

Hands-on time: 5 minutes
Cooking time: 5 minutes

400g (14oz) fresh or frozen peas
grated zest and juice of 1 lemon
2 tbsp extra virgin olive oil
1–1½ tbsp wholegrain mustard, to taste
a small handful of fresh mint,
   roughly chopped
a large handful of rocket, torn
salt and freshly ground black pepper

1 Fill a large bowl with iced water. Bring a large pan of water to the boil, then add the peas, bring back to the boil and cook for 1 minute. Drain the peas, then plunge them into the iced water to cool. Drain and put into a bowl.

2 Put the lemon zest and juice, oil and mustard with some seasoning into a jug and whisk together.

3 Toss the dressing, mint and rocket through the peas. Check the seasoning and serve as a side dish.

SAVE TIME

Prepare the salad to the end of step 2 up to one day ahead. Cover the peas and dressing separately with clingfilm. Complete the recipe to serve.

140

Serves 6

Sticky Toffee Pudding

Hands-on time: 20 minutes
Cooking time: about 35 minutes

For the sponge

200g (7oz) dates, stoned and
    finely chopped
250ml (9fl oz) tea, freshly brewed
125g (4oz) butter, softened, plus extra
    to grease
250g (9oz) self-raising flour, plus extra
    to dust
200g (7oz) light brown muscovado
    sugar
2 tbsp golden syrup
3 medium eggs
1 tsp bicarbonate of soda

For the toffee sauce

200ml (7fl oz) double cream
75g (3oz) light brown muscovado
    sugar
25g (1oz) butter
1 tbsp golden syrup

1 Preheat the oven to 180°C (160°C fan
    oven) mark 4. Put the dates into a
    bowl, pour the hot tea over them
    and leave to soak for 10 minutes.

SAVE TIME

Prepare the pudding to the end of
step 3 up to one day ahead. Leave
the sponge to cool completely in the
tin, then cover and store at room
temperature. Transfer the toffee
sauce to a bowl and leave to cool,
then cover and chill. To serve, reheat
the sponge in a preheated 180°C
(160°C fan oven) mark 4 oven for 15
minutes, if you like, and gently warm
the sauce in a pan.

Grease a 25.5 × 20.5cm (10 × 8in)
roasting tin, dust with flour and tap
out the excess.

2 To make the sponge, put the butter
    and sugar into a large bowl and beat
    together using a hand-held electric
    whisk until light and fluffy – about 5
    minutes. Whisk in the golden syrup,

Serves 6–8

followed by the eggs, bicarbonate of soda, flour and the date mixture (it may look a little curdled, but don't worry). Pour the mixture into the prepared tin and bake for 30–35 minutes until a skewer inserted into the centre comes out clean.

3 Meanwhile, make the toffee sauce: put all the ingredients into a pan and heat gently until melted and smooth, then increase the heat and simmer gently for 5 minutes.

4 Serve warm or at room temperature, with the toffee sauce.

Very British Buffet

Elderflower Cordial

To make about 1.1 litres (2 pints), you will need:

2kg (4½lb) golden granulated sugar, 80g (just over 3oz) citric acid , 2 medium lemons, sliced and 20 large young elderflower heads (shake to release any insects).

1 Bring 1.1 litres (2 pints) water to the boil, add the sugar and stir until dissolved.
2 Add the citric acid and lemon slices. Stir in the flower heads. Leave overnight, covered.
3 In the morning sieve. If you want it clearer, strain again through muslin or a coffee filter. Bottle, give some away and keep the rest in the fridge – it will last for months!

'Still' Lemonade

To make about 1.1 litres (2 pints), you will need:

3 lemons and 175g (6oz) sugar.

1 Remove the lemon zest thinly with a potato peeler.
2 Put the zest and sugar into a bowl or large jug and pour on 900ml (1½ pints) boiling water. Cover and leave to cool, stirring occasionally.
3 Add the juice of the lemons and strain the lemonade. Serve chilled.

Cranberry Cooler

To serve one you will need:
ice cubes, 75ml (2½fl oz) cranberry juice, lemonade or sparkling water, chilled and 1 lemon slice to serve.

1 Half-fill a tall glass with ice and pour in the cranberry juice.
2 Top up with lemonade. If you'd prefer the drink to be less sweet, double the amount of cranberry juice and top up with sparkling water. Stir well and serve with a slice of lemon.

Fruity Punch

To serve 12 you will need:
1 litre (1¾ pints) apple juice, chilled,
1 litre (1¾ pints) ginger ale, chilled,
2 apples, sliced and cut into stars, or star fruit, thinly sliced.

1 Put the apple juice, ginger ale and apple shapes in a large bowl and mix well.
2 Pour into a large jug and serve.

Fruity Carrot with Ginger

To serve 400ml (14 fl oz) you will need:
2 medium oranges, 1cm (½in) piece fresh root ginger, peeled and roughly chopped, 150ml (¼ pint) freshly pressed apple juice or 2 dessert apples, juiced, 150ml (¼ pint) freshly pressed carrot juice or 3 medium carrots, 250g (9oz), juiced and mint leaves to decorate.

1 Using a sharp knife, cut a slice of orange and put to one side for the decoration. Cut off the peel from the oranges, removing as much of the white pith as possible. Chop the flesh roughly, discarding any pips, and put into a blender. Add the chopped ginger.
2 Pour in the apple and carrot juice and blend until smooth. Divide between two glasses, decorate with quartered orange slices and a mint leaf and serve.

Stress-free get-ahead time plan

Up to two days ahead
- Make the Salmon Sandwich Stacks.
- Make the Triumphant Strawberry and Cream Jelly.

Up to one day ahead
- Make the Coronation Chicken (but don't add the coriander or garnish).
- Make the Layered Omelette Cake.
- Make the Cheese and Pickle Crown Bread.
- Prepare The Perfect Victoria Sponge.
- Prepare the Individual Queen of Trifles.

On the day

5 hours before you serve
- Prepare the Individual Sausage and Egg Pies and cook now – or closer to serving time if you want them warm

4 hours before you serve
- Make the Marmite Cheese Straws.

2 hours before you serve
- Prepare the Light and Fresh Potato Salad (but don't add the cress).
- Slice the salmon stacks. Chill.

30 minutes before you serve
- Complete the Coronation Chicken.
- Add the cress to the potato salad.
- Finish off the Victoria sponge and trifles.

When your guests arrive
- Hand round the nibbles.
- Serve the main courses when you're ready!
- Remember to turn out the jelly before you serve the puddings.

Buffet Menu for 12

Salmon Sandwich Stacks
Marmite Cheese Straws

*

Coronation Chicken
Individual Sausage and Egg Pies
Layered Omelette Cake
Light and Fresh Potato Salad
Cheese and Pickle Crown Bread

*

The Perfect Victoria Sponge
Individual Queen of Trifles
Triumphant Strawberry and Cream Jelly

Salmon Sandwich Stacks

Hands-on time: 10 minutes, plus chilling

500g (1lb 2oz) mascarpone cheese
1 tbsp roughly chopped capers
finely grated zest and juice of 1 lemon
2 tbsp freshly chopped dill
1 tbsp milk
12 medium-cut slices white bread
350g (12oz) smoked salmon slices

1 Put the mascarpone, capers, lemon zest and juice, dill and milk into a large bowl and mix well. Lay the bread on a board and divide half the mascarpone mixture among the slices. Spread evenly to the edges of the bread.

2 Next, divide half the smoked salmon slices over the mascarpone, making sure the fish is in an even layer (use scissors to trim). Lay another piece of bread on top of each stack and repeat the process with the remaining mascarpone mixture, smoked salmon and bread. Wrap the stacks individually in clingfilm and chill for at least 5 hours, or ideally overnight.

3 Using a large serrated knife, cut the crusts off the sandwich stacks, then slice each stack into six rectangles. Secure each stack with a cocktail stick, if you like, and serve.

SAVE TIME

Stack, wrap and chill the sandwiches up to two days ahead. Slice the stacks into rectangles up to 2 hours ahead and keep chilled. Serve when ready.

Makes 24

Marmite Cheese Straws

Hands-on time: 10 minutes
Cooking time: about 20 minutes

2 × 375g sheets ready-rolled puff pastry
plain flour to dust
1½ tbsp Marmite
1½ tbsp milk
75g (3oz) each finely grated Parmesan
  and Gruyère

1 Preheat the oven to 200°C (180°C fan oven) mark 6. Line baking sheets with baking parchment.

2 Unroll one puff pastry sheet on to a lightly floured worksurface. Put the Marmite into a small bowl and gradually mix in the milk. Brush half the mixture over the pastry.

3 Put both cheeses into another small bowl and stir to combine, then sprinkle half the cheese mixture over the pastry. Unroll the second puff pastry sheet and place on top of the cheese. Lightly roll a rolling pin over the pastry to stick the sheets together, rolling the pastry a little thinner in the process. Brush the top with the remaining

Marmite mixture, then sprinkle the remaining cheese over the top (pressing the cheese down to help it stick). Cut the pastry lengthways into 12 equal long strips, then halve to make 24 shorter strips.

4 Transfer the strips to the prepared baking sheets and cook for 15–20 minutes until golden brown. Transfer to a wire rack. Serve warm or at room temperature.

SAVE TIME

Make the cheese straws up to 4 hours ahead.

Makes 24

Coronation Chicken

🍴 **Hands-on time:** 20 minutes
Cooking time: about 20 minutes, plus cooling

6 skinless chicken breasts
2 tsp mild curry powder
150g (5oz) mayonnaise
125g (4oz) crème fraîche
3 tbsp mango chutney
1 tsp Worcestershire sauce
2 celery sticks, finely chopped
75g (3oz) dried ready-to-eat apricots, chopped
50g (2oz) sultanas
50g (2oz) flaked almonds
a large handful of fresh coriander, chopped
salt and freshly ground black pepper

SAVE TIME

Prepare the chicken to the end of step 3 up to one day ahead, but don't add the coriander or garnish. Cover with clingfilm and chill. To serve, stir the chopped coriander through and complete the recipe.

1 Put the chicken breasts into a large pan and cover with cold water. Bring to the boil, then reduce the heat and simmer gently for 15 minutes or until the chicken is cooked through (slice a breast in half to check). Drain and leave until completely cool.

2 Meanwhile, heat a small frying pan and toast the curry powder, stirring, until it smells fragrant – about 30 seconds. Empty into a large bowl and stir in the next seven ingredients, along with plenty of seasoning.

3 Cut or rip the cooled chicken into bite-size pieces and add to the mayonnaise mixture, along with most of the flaked almonds and chopped coriander. Stir well and check the seasoning.

4 To serve, garnish with the remaining almonds and coriander.

154

Serves 12

Individual Sausage and Egg Pies

Hands-on time: 30 minutes
Cooking time: about 40 minutes, plus cooling

7 small eggs
450g (1lb) sausage meat
1 tbsp wholegrain mustard
2 spring onions, finely chopped
1 tsp dried mixed herbs
plain flour to dust
about 1kg (2¼lb) shortcrust pastry
salt and freshly ground black pepper

1 Bring a large pan of water to the boil and add six of the eggs. Reduce the heat and simmer for exactly 6 minutes. Lift out of the pan with a slotted spoon and run them under cold water to cool. Put to one side.

2 Put the sausage meat, mustard, spring onions, mixed herbs and some seasoning into a large bowl and mix well. Put to one side.

3 Preheat the oven to 220°C (200°C fan oven) mark 7. Lightly dust a worksurface with flour and roll out two-thirds of the pastry to 3mm (⅛in) thick. Stamp out twelve 10cm (4in) circles and press the circles into 12 holes of a deep muffin tin, working the pastry so that it comes just above the edges of the holes. Put the trimmings to one side.

4 Carefully shell the eggs and halve lengthways through the yolk (which should not yet be completely set). Position one egg half, cut side down, in the bottom of each pastry well. Divide the sausage mixture among the wells, carefully pushing it around the eggs and levelling the surface.

5 Roll out the remaining one-third of pastry and trimmings as before and stamp out 7.5cm (3in) circles. Lightly beat the remaining egg and brush the edges of the filled pies and the visible sausage meat with some of the beaten egg, then press on the lids and seal the edges firmly. Use a skewer to pierce a hole in the centre of each lid to allow steam to escape. If you like, re-roll any trimmings and use to decorate the pies. Brush the top of the pies with egg.

Makes 12

6 Cook the pies for 30–35 minutes until deep golden brown. Cool for 5 minutes in the tin, then remove from the tin and transfer the pies to a baking tray. Cook for 5 minutes more to crisp up the edges.

7 Cool for 10 minutes, then serve warm or at room temperature.

Layered Omelette Cake

Hands-on time: 30 minutes, plus chilling
Cooking time: about 25 minutes

16 large eggs
5 tbsp freshly chopped chives
2 tbsp vegetable oil
500g (1lb 2oz) full-fat cream cheese
1 red pepper, seeded and finely diced
½ red chilli, seeded and finely
   chopped (see Safety Tip, page 52)
50g (2oz) watercress, chopped, plus
   extra to garnish
salt and freshly ground black pepper

1 Beat the eggs in a large jug with
   2 tbsp of the chives and plenty of
   seasoning. Heat ½ tbsp of the oil
   in a 20.5cm (8in) non-stick frying
   pan and pour in a quarter of the egg
   mixture. Swirl the pan to ensure the
   base is covered. Using a spatula,
   occasionally push the mixture in
   from the sides of the pan while it's
   cooking (but ensuring the base is
   always fully covered with egg).
   Cook for 2–3 minutes until the
   underneath is golden, then flip
   the omelette and cook for 2–3
   minutes more. Transfer to a plate
   to cool completely.

2 Repeat with the remaining oil and
   egg mixture to make three more
   omelettes (you may need to whisk
   the eggs before making each
   omelette to redistribute the chives).

3 While the omelettes are cooling,
   beat together the cream cheese,
   remaining chives, the red pepper,
   chilli, chopped watercress and some
   seasoning in a large bowl. Line a
   20.5cm (8in) cake tin with clingfilm
   and place a cooled omelette in the
   base. Spread a third of the cream

SAVE TIME

Prepare the omelette cake to the
end of step 3 up to one day ahead.
Chill. Complete the recipe to serve.

Serves 12

cheese mixture over the omelette. Repeat the stacking and spreading twice more and then top with the remaining omelette. Cover the tin with clingfilm and chill in the fridge for at least 30 minutes.

4 To serve, lift the omelette cake from the tin and peel off the clingfilm. Transfer to a serving plate or cake stand, garnish with watercress and serve in wedges.

Light and Fresh Potato Salad

Hands-on time: 15 minutes
Cooking time: about 25 minutes

1.5kg (3lb 2oz) new potatoes, unpeeled, chopped into bite-size pieces
100ml (3½fl oz) olive oil
2 tbsp wholegrain mustard
juice of ½ lemon
200g (7oz) radishes, thinly sliced
4 spring onions, thinly sliced
a punnet of cress
salt and freshly ground black pepper

1 Cook the potatoes in salted boiling water for 15–20 minutes until just tender but not breaking apart.
2 While the potatoes are cooking, whisk together the oil, mustard, lemon juice and plenty of seasoning.
3 Drain the potatoes and leave to steam-dry for 5 minutes, then put them back into the pan. Pour the dressing over and add the radishes and spring onions. Fold together, trying not to break up the potatoes.
4 Tip into a serving dish and scatter the leaves from a punnet of cress over the top.

SAVE TIME

Prepare the potato salad up to a couple of hours ahead, but do not add the cress. Transfer to a serving dish, cover with clingfilm and chill. Complete the recipe to serve.

Serves 12

Cheese and Pickle Crown Bread

Hands-on time: 30 minutes, plus rising
Cooking time: about 30 minutes, plus cooling

25g (1oz) butter
300ml (½ pint) milk
2 medium eggs
450g (1lb) strong plain flour, plus extra
   to dust
1 tsp caster sugar
7g sachet fast-action yeast
1 tsp salt
150g (5oz) Branston pickle
150g (5oz) extra mature Cheddar,
   grated
oil to grease

1 Heat the butter in a small pan until melted, then stir in the milk and heat gently for 1 minute until just warm. Beat in one of the eggs.

2 Put the flour, sugar, yeast and salt into a bowl and stir together. Add the milk mixture and stir quickly to make a soft, but not sticky, dough (add a little more milk/flour as needed). Tip the dough on to a lightly floured worksurface and knead for 10 minutes. Form into a ball, cover with a clean teatowel and leave to rise for 30 minutes.

3 Roll the dough out to make a 25.5 × 38cm (10 × 15in) rectangle. Put the pickle and cheese into a small bowl and stir to mix, then spread the mixture over the dough, leaving a 1cm (½in) border. Roll the dough up from one of the long edges to make a sausage shape. Use a bread knife to cut into 12 slices. Flour a baking sheet, then arrange the slices on their sides (with the swirls facing

SAVE TIME

Prepare the salad to the end of
step 2 up to one day ahead. Cover
the peas and dressing separately
with clingfilm. Complete the recipe
to serve.

Serves 12

sideways) and just touching to make
a ring shape on the baking sheet.
Loosely cover with oiled clingfilm
and leave to rise for 30 minutes.

4 Preheat the oven to 200°C (180°C
fan oven) mark 6. Beat the

remaining egg and use to glaze the
rolls. Bake for 25–30 minutes until
risen, golden and the rolls feel firm.
Transfer to a wire rack and cool
completely.

The Perfect Victoria Sponge

Hands-on time: 30 minutes
Cooking time: about 30 minutes, plus cooling

225g (8oz) unsalted butter, softened, plus extra to grease

225g (8oz) self-raising flour, plus extra to dust

225g (8oz) caster sugar

4 medium eggs

1 tbsp milk

6 tbsp loose strawberry jam

250ml (8fl oz) double cream

icing sugar to dust

SAVE TIME

Prepare the sponges to the end of step 4 up to one day ahead. Wrap the cooled sponges in clingfilm and store at room temperature. Complete the recipe up to 2 hours ahead.

1 Preheat the oven to 180°C (160°C fan oven) mark 4. Lightly grease two 20.5cm (8in) sandwich tins and line the bases with baking parchment. Dust the sides of each tin with flour and tap out the excess.

2 Put the butter and caster sugar into a large bowl and beat together using a hand-held electric whisk until pale and fluffy – about 3 minutes. Gradually add the eggs, beating well after each addition (if the mixture looks as if it might curdle, mix in a few tbsp of the flour).

3 Sift in the flour and fold together using a large metal spoon. Next, fold in the milk.

4 Divide the mixture equally between the prepared tins and level the surface of each. Bake in the centre of the oven for 25–30 minutes until the cakes are golden and springy to the touch when lightly pressed in the centre. Leave the cakes to cool in the tins for 5 minutes, then turn out,

Cuts into 10 slices

transfer to a wire rack and leave to cool completely.

5 Peel off the lining papers. Spread the jam over the top of one of the sponge cakes. Next, lightly whip the cream in a medium bowl and dollop over the jam layer. Top with the remaining sponge cake and dust with icing sugar. Serve in slices.

Individual Queen of Trifles

Hands-on time: 30 minutes, plus chilling
Cooking time: about 10 minutes, plus cooling

300g (11oz) Madeira sponge cake
25–40ml (1–1½fl oz) cream sherry, to
   taste, or orange juice
5 tbsp raspberry jam
300g (11oz) raspberries
4 tbsp custard powder
4 tbsp caster sugar
600ml (1 pint) milk
2 tsp vanilla extract
300ml (½ pint) double cream
2 tbsp icing sugar, sifted
about 50g (2oz) meringue nests,
   crumbled
25g (1oz) shelled unsalted pistachios,
   chopped

SAVE TIME

Prepare the trifles to the end of step
4 up to one day ahead. Complete
the recipe up to 1 hour ahead.

1 Slice the Madeira cake into 10 equal
  slices and roughly crumble each slice
  into the bottom of a tumbler or small
  wine glass. Press down lightly. Divide
  the sherry or orange juice among the
  glasses, pouring it over the cake.

2 Heat the jam gently in a medium
  pan until it loosens. Add the fresh
  raspberries and gently stir to coat
  the berries in the jam. Divide among
  the glasses.

3 Next, make the custard. Put the
  custard powder and caster sugar
  into a pan and gradually whisk in
  the milk until smooth. Put the pan
  over a medium heat and bring to the
  boil, stirring constantly to prevent

Makes 10

lumps, then cook until the custard thickens. Take off the heat and stir in the vanilla extract. Leave to cool for 15 minutes.

4 Re-whisk the custard to break it up and divide among the glasses. Chill until needed.

5 To serve, lightly whip the cream and icing sugar until the cream just holds its shape. Divide among the glasses, then scatter the meringues and pistachios on top. Serve.

Triumphant Strawberry and Cream Jelly

Hands-on time: 20 minutes, plus chilling
Cooking time: about 5 minutes, plus cooling

2 × 135g packs strawberry jelly
1 tsp edible gold glitter (optional)
oil for greasing (optional)
100g (3½oz) caster sugar
1 vanilla pod, split lengthways
300ml (½ pint) double cream
600ml (1 pint) milk
8 gelatine sheets

1 Snip the jelly into cubes and put into a large jug. Pour in 300ml (½ pint) boiling water and leave to dissolve, stirring occasionally. Top up the mixture with cold water to make 1.2 litres (2 pints). Stir in the glitter, if you like.

2 Pour the strawberry jelly mixture into a 2.7 litre (4¾ pint) non-stick kugelhopf mould or large bowl (if your bowl or mould is not non-stick, grease lightly with a mild oil). Chill until completely set – about 3 hours.

3 Meanwhile, put the sugar, vanilla pod, cream and milk into a pan and heat gently, whisking occasionally to help release the vanilla seeds, until the mixture just begins to boil. Take off the heat and leave to infuse for 15 minutes.

4 Put the gelatine sheets into a bowl, cover with cold water and leave to soak for 5 minutes. Lift the soaked gelatine out of the water (discard the water) and add to the cream pan, then stir to dissolve (if the cream mixture is not hot enough to dissolve the gelatine, then reheat gently until it dissolves). Lift out the vanilla pod and leave the cream mixture until completely cool – the strawberry jelly needs to be fully set before proceeding.

5 Gently pour the cream mixture over the set jelly and chill to set completely – about 5 hours.

6 To serve, turn the jelly out on to a serving plate. If it doesn't come out easily, dip the base of the mould

Serves 10

briefly into a bowl of hot water
(taking care no water comes in
contact with the jelly). Turn out
and serve.

SAVE TIME

Make the jelly to the end of step
5 up to two days ahead. Chill.
Complete the recipe to serve.

137 cal ♥ 3g protein
6g fat (1g sat) ♥ 3g fibre
19g carb ♥ 0.1g salt

10

92 cal ♥ 1g protein
8g fat (1g sat) ♥ 1g fibre
5g carb ♥ 0.1g salt

12

470 cal ♥ 25g protein
20g fat (2.5g sat) ♥ 9g fibre
49g carb ♥ 2.5g salt

14

313 cal ♥ 6g protein ♥ 26g fat
(5g sat) ♥ 3g fibre
14g carb ♥ 0.6

16

98 cal ♥ 3g protein
5g fat (2g sat) ♥ 1g fibre
11g carb ♥ 0.2g salt

30

197 cal ♥ 14g protein
16g fat (4g sat) ♥ 6g fibre
5g carb ♥ 1.3g salt

32

332 cal ♥ 7g protein
20g fat (6g sat) ♥ 1g fibre
28g carb ♥ 2g salt

34

37 cal ♥ 7g protein
2g fat (trace sat) ♥ 0g fibre
0g carb ♥ 0.2g salt

52

291 cal ♥ 31g protein
17g fat (3g sat) ♥ 1g fibre
2g carb ♥ 3g salt

54

180 cal ♥ 27g protein
8g fat (2g sat) ♥ 0g fibre
trace carb ♥ 0.1g salt

56

220 cal ♥ 13g protein
8g fat (2g sat) ♥ 1g fibre
7g carb ♥ 0.3g salt

68

710 cal ♥ 34g protein
48g fat (9g sat) ♥ 2g fibre
37g carb ♥ 1.7g salt

72

322 cal ♥ 44g protein
23g fat (9g sat) ♥ 0g fibre
trace carb ♥ 0.3g salt

74

579 cal ♥ 69g protein
34g fat (15g sat) ♥ 0g fibre
0g carb ♥ 0.4g salt

78

Calorie Gallery

346 cal ♥ 9g protein
13g fat (5g sat) ♥ 9g fibre
40g carb ♥ 2.2g salt

18

382 cal ♥ 9g protein
27g fat (8g sat) ♥ 3g fibre
25g carb ♥ 2.5g salt

20

296 cal ♥ 19g protein
14g fat (3g sat) ♥ 4g fibre
23g carb ♥ 2.3g salt

24

408 cal ♥ 11g protein
15g fat (2g sat) ♥ 1g fibre
48g carb ♥ 1.3g salt

28

413 cal ♥ 3g protein
38g fat (5g sat) ♥ 3g fibre
16g carb ♥ 0.1g salt

36

381 cal ♥ 23g protein
29g fat (17g sat) ♥ 3g fibre
8g carb ♥ 1.5g salt

38

450 cal ♥ 6g protein
40g fat (4g sat) ♥ 5g fibre
16g carb ♥ 0.3g salt

40

290 cal ♥ 32g protein
18g fat (3g sat) ♥ 0g fibre
0.1g carb ♥ 0.6g salt

48

409 cal ♥ 49g protein
23g fat (5g sat) ♥ 3g fibre
13g carb ♥ 0.5g salt

58

330 cal ♥ 55g protein
8g fat (1g sat) ♥ 1g fibre
19g carb ♥ 0.3g salt

62

135 cal ♥ 13g protein
6g fat (1g sat) ♥ 0g fibre
trace carb ♥ 0.2g salt

64

257 cal ♥ 29g protein
14g fat (4g sat) ♥ 0g fibre
13g carb ♥ 0.5g salt

66

310 cal ♥ 24g protein
20g fat (8g sat) ♥ 0g fibre
3g carb ♥ 0.8g salt

80

789 cal ♥ 20g protein
52g fat (17g sat) ♥ 4g fibre
58g carb ♥ 4g salt

82

164 cal ♥ 7g protein
13g fat (5g sat) ♥ 1g fibre
7g carb ♥ 1.1g salt

86

138 cal ♥ 10g protein
11g fat (5g sat) ♥ 4g fibre
4g carb ♥ 1.2g salt

88

91 cal ♥ 1g protein
6g fat (trace sat) ♥ 1g fibre
9g carb ♥ trace salt

90

629 cal ♥ 48g protein
38g fat (15g sat) ♥ 2g fibre
27g carb ♥ 3.5g salt

94

718 cal ♥ 49g protein
39g fat (18g sat) ♥ 1g fibre
45g carb ♥ 2.3g salt

96

511 cal ♥ 42g protein
30g fat (10g sat) ♥ 1g fibre
19g carb ♥ 2.5g salt

100

489 cal ♥ 34g protein
22g fat (10g sat) ♥ 2g fibre
40g carb ♥ 1.2g salt

114

499 cal ♥ 21g protein
15g fat (3g sat) ♥ 9g fibre
75g carb ♥ 1.7g salt

116

253 cal ♥ 8g protein
18g fat (3g sat) ♥ 1g fibre
16g carb ♥ 0.8g salt

118

253 cal ♥ 8g protein
18g fat (3g sat) ♥ 2g fibre
15g carb ♥ 0.2g salt

120

548 cal ♥ 20g protein
39g fat (23g sat) ♥ 1g fibre
29g carb ♥ 0.4g salt

134

204 cal ♥ 9g protein
10g fat (6g sat) ♥ 1g fibre
20g carb ♥ 0.8g salt

136

125 cal ♥ 3g protein
7g fat (1g sat) ♥ 3g fibre
13g carb ♥ 0.4g salt

138

83 cal ♥ 5g protein
5g fat (1g sat) ♥ 3g fibre
7g carb ♥ 0.4g salt

140

508 cal ♥ 13g protein
35g fat (28g sat) ♥ 2g fibre
37g carb ♥ 2.0g salt

156

321 cal ♥ 12g protein
31g fat (15g sat) ♥ 0.3g fibre
1g carb ♥ 0.8g salt

158

149 cal ♥ 3g protein
7g fat (1g sat) ♥ 2g fibre
21g carb ♥ 0.3g salt

160

239 cal ♥ 10g protein
8g fat (4g sat) ♥ 1g fibre
34g carb 1.2g salt

162

281 cal ♥ 36g protein
12g fat (3g sat) ♥ 0g fibre
8g carb ♥ 1.0g salt

102

623 cal ♥ 39g protein
39g fat (13g sat) ♥ 1g fibre
29g carb ♥ 1.8g salt

106

587 cal ♥ 48g protein
24g fat (6g sat) ♥ 1g fibre
47g carb ♥ 2.0g salt

108

293 cal ♥ 33g protein
10g fat (2g sat) ♥ 1g fibre
19g carb ♥ 1.1g salt

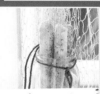

110

without topping:
165 cal ♥ 8g protein
6g fat (3g sat) ♥ 1g fibre
22g carb ♥ 0.5g salt

126

148 cal ♥ 0g protein
0g fat ♥ 0g fibre
39g carb ♥ 0g salt

128

406 cal ♥ 7g protein
33g fat (17g sat) ♥ 1g fibre
21g carb ♥ 2.3g salt

130

130 cal ♥ 4g protein
9g fat (6g sat) ♥ 0.6g fibre
10g carb ♥ 0.3g salt

132

for 8 servings: 637 cal
6g protein ♥ 32g fat (10g sat)
1g fibre ♥ 88g carb ♥ 0.7g salt
for 6 servings: 849 cal
8g protein ♥ 43g fat (13g sat)
2g fibre ♥ 117g carb ♥ 0.9g salt

142

140 cal ♥ 6g protein
11g fat (6g sat) ♥ 0.3g fibre
6g carb ♥ 0.8g salt

150

150 cal ♥ 4g protein
10g fat (7g sat) ♥ 0.2g fibre
11g carb ♥ 0.5g salt

152

292 cal ♥ 21g protein
19g fat (5g sat) ♥ 0.8g fibre
10g carb ♥ 0.7g salt

154

527 cal ♥ 5g protein
35g fat (21g sat) ♥ 0.5g fibre
52g carb ♥ 0.5g salt

164

229 cal ♥ 5g protein
6g fat (3g sat) ♥ 1g fibre
43g carb ♥ 0.4g salt

166

294 cal ♥ 5g protein
17g fat (11g sat) ♥ 0g fibre
31g carb ♥ 0.1g salt

168

Index

PICTURE CREDITS

Photographers: Nicki Dowey
(pages 13, 17, 21, 29, 33, 35, 49,
53, 55, 57, 59, 63, 65, 67, 69, 73, 75,
79, 81, 83, 87, 89, 91, 95 and 121);
Gareth Morgans (pages 11, 19 and
25); Myles New (pages 97, 101, 103,
105, 107, 109, 111, 115, 117, 119, 127,
129, 131, 133, 135, 137, 139, 141, 143,
151, 153, 155, 157, 159, 161, 163, 165,
167 and 169); Craig Robertson
(pages 8, 9, 51, 60, 70 and 98);
Lucinda Symons (pages 37, 39
and 41); Kate Whitaker (pages 15
and 31).

Home Economists:
Joanna Farrow, Emma Jane Frost,
Teresa Goldfinch, Alice Hart,
Lucy McKelvie, Kim Morphew,
Aya Nishimura, Bridget Sargeson,
Kate Trend and Mari Mereid
Williams.

Stylists: Tamzin Ferdinando,
Wei Tang, Helen Trent and
Fanny Ward

BAKE ME A CAKE
There's always time for cake

EASY PEASY MEALS
Easy meals for every day

LET'S DO BRUNCH
Mouth-watering meals to start your day

CHEAP EATS
Budget-busting ideas that won't break the bank

SALAD DAYS
Oh-so-fresh ideas for fabulous salads

Available online at store.anovabooks.com and from all good bookshops

POSH NOSH
Delicious recipes to impress your guests

PARTY FOOD
Delicious recipes to get the party started

SLOW STOPPERS
Slow-cooked meals packed with flavour

GREAT VEG
Inspired ideas for delicious veggie meals

AL FRESCO EATS
Easy grills, barbecues and picnics

ROAST IT
There's nothing better than a delicious roast

FLASH IN THE PAN
Spice up your noodles and stir-fries

GLUTEN-FREE AND EASY
Oh-so-good-for-you recipes that taste great

LOW FAT LOW CAL
Nice recipes don't need to be naughty